SHC

Shoot a Line

A MERCHANT MARINER'S WAR

by

Captain Denis Foss MN
with
Basil Entwistle

LindenHall

PUBLISHED 1992
BY LINDEN HALL
223 PRESTON ROAD, YEOVIL
SOMERSET BA20 2EW

COPIES AVAILABLE FROM
TIRLEY GARTH, TARPOLEY,
CHESHIRE CW6 0LZ

ISBN 0 948747 11 0

COVER DESIGN BY W. CAMERON JOHNSON
PHOTOTYPESETTING BY INTYPE, LONDON
PRINTED BY BIDDLES OF GUILDFORD,
ENGLAND

BASIL ENTWISTLE graduated from Oxford University with first class honours in philosophy, politics and economics. He left a teaching career to work in the field of human and social development, spending eight years in Japan at the invitation of postwar leaders to participate in the country's democratic regeneration and authored *Japan's Decisive Decade*. During World War II he served in Europe at US Air Force headquarters editing publications. In the 1960s he returned to education as founder and first chair of Mackinac College. He now lives with his wife in Santa Barbara, California.

Contents

A personal word

I would like to express my heartfelt gratitude to my wife Nancy and to all who have made this book possible. In particular to Basil Entwistle who took thousands of my words and licked them into shape; to my brother Patrick and his wife Margaret; to John and Jeanne Faber who constantly encouraged me and handled the production; to Bill Cameron Johnson who designed the cover; to the typesetters and printers – and a host of friends who have helped bring this book to birth.

I wish to dedicate it to the men of the Merchant Navy, whose courage, resilience and sacrifices in the last war may not always have received the recognition they deserve.

DENIS FOSS

Foreword

Denis Foss stands six feet four inches tall and is an outstanding man in other respects. His exploits as a merchant mariner all through World War II make an epic tale. Several times he cheated death; he helped pioneer the means to speed up the crucial servicing of ships of war. As he went about his business he also made himself at home on five continents and gained a host of friends in many lands.

Denis is a big hearted character who jumps in where angels fear to tread; as a result his adventures are spiced with encounters with people who make the wheels go round – Abdul Gammer Nasser of Egypt, the Governor-General and two prime ministers of Australia. Somehow he contrived to bring together management and labour to heal a bitter conflict which threatened the war effort of one nation. As a second mate he found himself advising admirals and cabinet ministers.

Woven through this tale is the moving account of a marriage often threatened by abrasive personalities and long separations, yet sustained by honesty and caring. Denis plunges beneath the surface of hectic action to portray a man wrestling with his doubts and fears, temptations and defeats. More than that, he reveals the secret of his strength – a simple faith which compels him to listen in the quiet of his heart and mind to the still small voice of God. The guidance from that source proved as vital for him in his human encounters as the compass with which he steered his ship amidst reefs and storms.

Here is a stirring yarn for seafarers, a revealing story for war veterans, and a human saga for every man and woman perplexed by today's cross currents of life. I feel privileged to have had a hand in writing it.

BASIL ENTWISTLE

Santa Barbara, August 1992

1

Green horn at sea

The worst that I had feared was finally happening. Glued to the radio, I was listening to Prime Minister Chamberlain announcing that Britain was at war with Germany. The news, shocking though it was, had not taken me by surprise. I had recently spent several months in Germany working to obtain a diploma in hotel management before taking a job in my family's hotel in Bournemouth. During my time in Germany I had seen enough to know that Hitler was taking every opportunity to stock arms, submarine parts and mobile weapons, produced by industries all over the Ruhr valley.

A big importer of goods from Germany had phoned me from London last month to say, "I'm told by my German contacts that war will break out in September, if not this year, next year." He had asked me to book rooms for himself and his key staff, and the whole hotel annexe as his head office, saying, "We're bound to be bombed out of our East End office before very long."

He had also advised me to buy black-out

materials, car tyres, torches, bicycle lights and reflectors and other items which he said would disappear off the war-time market. And he added, "Why not use German industries to build our stocks for winning the war?"

But the actual declaration of war shook me up. I was twenty-three, and along with my generation had to come to grips with what my part should be in the defence of my country. During the next few weeks I went through a lot of turmoil. I had made many German friends and was haunted by the nightmare of having to kill one of them if we met in combat. My ideas of warfare were shaped by tales of the trenches and bayonet charges of World War I and my spirit shrank from them.

Besides these fears, I had married a couple of years earlier and hated the idea of leaving my wife Nancy and our little daughter. But I had also served as a young fellow in the Merchant Service after studying at Pangbourne Nautical College. So I finally decided to apply to the Royal Navy.

When an examining officer looked through my medical records he laughed. During one of my escapades I'd had an accident and broken my back. With that in my records, he said, he doubted if I would ever be accepted in one of the services.

I had the same response when I applied to join the Air Force. I had no stomach for the Army, with my visions of rushing out to stick a bayonet into someone's guts. On the other hand, my conscience would not allow me just to work in a hotel or a factory. After being turned down at several recruiting offices I went up to London and applied at the Shipping Federation to rejoin the Merchant Service.

I walked down Connaught Road to the Federation Office on the Royal Docks and told a clerk about my experience as a seaman. He took me to a Mr Jackson, the manager. I repeated my story and he told me to wait and he would see what he could do. I waited for five hours, missing lunch, and was hungry, bored and worried by the time he called to me in to his office. There he handed me a letter to take to the SS *Royal Star*, which was berthed in the Royal Victoria Dock. He said nothing about the job for which I was applying.

By the time I reached the ship it was 5 o'clock and the only officer on board was a Mr Roberts, the second mate. Roberts read the letter and said, "Bad luck, old man, we've just appointed a fourth mate, so there's no job for you here." I thought to myself, fourth mate; I'd never dreamed of such an important post.

Roberts looked at the letter again and asked me more about my seafaring experience; then he said, "Come with me. I'll phone the office and see if they have any other vacancies." As he talked in the telephone kiosk on the dock I heard him say, "Another fourth mate just turned up, a good type" – he winked at me – "he went to Pangbourne Nautical College, served his time with the New Zealand Shipping Company. Just the sort we need."

Roberts came out and grinned; "That's worked the trick. The superintendent wants to see you at eleven tomorrow morning. You be there on time and you'll be all right."

I thanked him and walked away, delighted at the possibility of returning to the sea, but little dreaming of the hair-raising adventures awaiting me during the next five years around the world.

Next morning, 23 December, 1939, I presented myself at the imposing Blue Star offices and was taken to see Captain Angus, the Marine Superintendent. "I'm sorry you missed the *Royal Star*," he said, "but I have another appointment, if you can make it. Could you join a ship three days from today? The third officer is on duty Christmas Day and wants to go home to see his wife next day, as the ship sails on the 27th."

I thought, that gives me Christmas Eve to get clothes and gear ready, a big job as I hadn't been near a ship in six years. I threw up a silent prayer and the thought came back, "Take the job." I said boldly, "Yes, I can be there Boxing Day."

"That's a weight off my mind," said Captain Angus. "Your ship is the *Avalona Star*, one of our best. You'll like her. She's much bigger and better fitted out than the *Royal*. She's also in the Royal Albert Dock. Perhaps I'll see you on board before she sails." Then he handed me over to his assistant, who asked to see my discharge papers – the book in which were entered the names of the ships in which you'd served, with a space for VG – very good ability and behaviour. I told him I'd never had a discharge book. He asked for my indentures as an apprentice. I told him lamely that I had no idea where they were.

"We can't take you on with no proof of your experience," he said firmly.

I got up to leave, feeling sick, when Captain

Angus looked up from his papers. "Which division were you in at Pangbourne?"

"Macquarie Division."

"And in which NZS ship did you serve your time, and who was its master?"

"The *Devon*, and Nobby Clarke was captain." Then I nearly bit my tongue for saying 'Nobby'.

Captain Angus laughed. "Join the *Avalona* on Boxing Day and we'll see if you're any good."

As I walked out of the office I thought, "That's a little miracle."

When I phoned Nancy, her response was, "Where will you go to get your kit in time?" A good question. I sat down on a bench near St Paul's Cathedral and addressed the Almighty in a desperate prayer – "I'm in a mess, God. Where do I go to get a uniform?" As though in answer, the thought came, "Moss Bros".

Well, I said to myself, they certainly rent clothes and must have all sizes in stock. Let's try. When I told a store assistant my dilemma, he replied that they didn't normally sell clothes, but he'd see what he could do. I was measured and soon he appeared with a naval suit, complete with Admiral's stripes on the arm and rows of medals. It fitted. They removed the stripes and medals.

Then they handed me the bill for an amount more than I had in my bank account. I gulped and wrote out a cheque. There was a pause while the manager was summoned. He said he was sorry they did not accept out of town cheques, then asked if I could give a couple of references who would vouch for me.

I reached around in my mind and put up another

prayer. Two names came to me – Sir Horace Wilson, Permanent Secretary at the Treasury, whom I knew as a guest at our family hotel, Linden Hall, and Austin Reed, the country's most famous men's outfitter, whom I had once met at a meeting. The manager looked impressed, went away for a few minutes and returned saying, "We'll accept your cheque, sir." Years later I learned that he had phoned both men and they had stood surety for me.

Back in Bournemouth that evening I was promptly piled high with work. The hotel had 180 Christmas guests and it was my responsibility to organise their entertainment, while Nancy spent half the night sewing name tabs on my new clothes. On Christmas Day I played Santa Claus and compered the fancy costume dance that night. Early next morning Nancy and I left for London.

As we stepped on to the Royal Albert Dock we were both overwhelmed by the size of RMS *Avalona Star* towering above us. Filled with apprehension, I struggled up the gangway, hauling my luggage. The ship seemed deserted. We walked around until we came on a sign, 'Officers' Accommodation'. All the doors were locked, until we reached one marked 'Third Officer'. The door swung open and third mate Seymour introduced himself. As soon as he learned that I was the new fourth mate he said, "Well, I'm off then; I just have time to catch my train to Bristol; I haven't been home yet for Christmas." As he picked up his bags he added, "There's an engineer, a donkeyman, one steward and a shore watchman on board.

Cheerio!" He gave me the key to my cabin and was on his way.

Nancy and I staggered in a daze to my cabin. It was small, but comfortable and well appointed. We decided to explore the ship. We found the bridge, everything locked up, and saw no one as we walked the boatdeck and accommodation deck and returned to my cabin. Soon there was a knock on the door and a cheerful young steward entered with a tray. "I thought you might like a cup of tea."

He then showed me the officers' pantry with food for supper left for me to cook for myself. We had just finished gratefully drinking our tea when there was another knock on the door. A smiling Irish face appeared. "I'm Tim Ryan, the shore bosun. The PLA (Port of London Authority) has just told us we must shift the ship tonight into the Royal Victoria Dock to complete the loading there."

"My God," I thought, "Here I am, in charge of this huge ship, no engines, no crew, and we have to shift ship! It's impossible."

Ryan evidently saw my turmoil and still smiling, said, "It's all right, Sir; I'll go forward, my mate Mick Lennon, will go aft, the donkeyman has put steam on deck, and there are two PLA men to shift the ropes. You go on the bridge and tell us what to do."

And that was what we did. Ropes had to be moved from a bollard on the starboard bow to a hundred feet on the port bow, the ropes aft slackened down to let the ship's bow be pulled out into the cutting between the two docks and the ship slowly but surely warped through to its new position. I was so overawed and everything was so strange I have no recollection of when Nancy took her leave. I spent an uneasy night worrying about whether I could handle this new job, how I would cope with unfamiliar people and circumstances, the fear of being torpedoed and drowning.

Next morning I watched this giant of a ship come to life. People arrived to continue the loading and the officers and crewmen of all sorts poured aboard. Many came to ask me questions as I stood near the gangway in my Moss Bros uniform. Not knowing the answers, I did my best to stall their queries. Eventually the Captain, 'Georgie' Hopper, came on board and sent for me.

"You the new fourth mate? I want you to stand at the head of the gangway and make sure no German agents come aboard. Stay there all day and check everyone who comes aboard."

As I stood obediently at the head of the gangway I wondered what a German agent looked like. People were coming and going all the time, storing ship, bringing cargo papers. I asked each one his business until chief officer Larry Evans told me to stop. Just standing there in my uniform, he said, should be enough! At day's end I fell into my bunk exhausted.

Next day we were due to sail. When third mate Seymour returned he was sent off by train to Southend to get our routing orders from the Admiralty Office, so I was left with the responsibility for the pre-sailing bridge checks. Every instrument on the bridge, the steering and engine room and telegraphs and telephone, had to be checked to be sure they were in order. This was something I knew nothing about. Luckily, in those days ships were hand-steered and we had on the bridge two quartermasters on each watch, experienced seamen who knew what needed to be done.

Two such men, Dalgleish and Galbraith, became my close friends. They came from the Hebrides and spoke to each other in Gaelic – the seamen called them North Sea Chinese. These two did all the testing for me this first day and I was able to report with confidence to the Master that everything was working.

When all our freight was loaded I was told to "go and get the draught". If I had ever known what that meant, I had forgotten. Once again I consulted my Gaelic friends and they led me down to the quay. We walked to each end of the ship and noted how deep she lay in the water, reading the depth marks. We then made the tugs fast, fore and aft, and two pilots came aboard, one each for the dock and the river, and the ship moved slowly off the quay. Back on the bridge I worked the telegraphs at the pilots' orders, carrying out the whispered instructions of Galbraith. To my relief *Avalona Star* made her way without incident through the locks and out on to the River Thames. We let go our tugs and were under way.

By this time it was seven o'clock, dinner time, and as fourth mate it was my duty to relieve the officers of the watch for their meal. So I was left on the bridge with the pilot and quartermaster until Captain Hopper came up and invited the pilot, named Middlemist, to join him below for a Christmas drink. As soon as the captain disap-

peared below, Middlemist went out quietly to the
end of the bridge, rolled up his sleeve, produced a
syringe and injected himself. I thought, "My God,
have I landed myself into a gang of drug addicts?"
It was only later that I learned that pilot Middlemist was a diabetic. He walked back to me and
said, "Keep her in the middle, sonny, she'll be all
right; there are no ships moving on the Thames
right now." And down he went.

A couple of minutes later it began to snow. I
couldn't see beyond the forecastle head of the ship.
I rushed to the telegraph and rang slow ahead. The
telephone rang; the pilot asked "Why did you ring
the telegraph?"

"It's snowing and I can't see very far ahead."

"Don't worry. You can see the river banks. The
quartermaster will keep her in the middle."

Of course he was right. He knew what he was
doing, but I didn't, and I was scared stiff. Was I
glad when I went down for my dinner!

At eight p.m. I was up on watch again and
shortly afterwards landed our pilot at Southend.
We still had several hours of steaming before we
were clear of sandbanks. The lighted buoys which
marked them had been halved in number because
of wartime, and their lights dimmed down. Out of
the murky night and through the snow flurries we
would suddenly see an unfamiliar silhouette. My
reaction – German E boats! Each time they turned
out to be the masts, funnels or upperworks of
ships sunk or grounded on sandbanks. It was an
immense relief at dawn to be well down Channel,
clear of sandbanks and headed, as we believed, for
Buenos Aires to load meat.

In those days on shipboard there was a deep sense of hierarchy. The captain spoke socially only with the chief engineer, the doctor, the purser and the passengers. On this ship the captain and chief engineer had fallen out with each other some years earlier and they never conversed, beyond passing niceties about the day and weather; they did their business by notes. Because the ship was large, the accommodations of deck officers and those of engineer officers were a distance apart, and so there were social cliques – deck and radio officers forward, under the bridge, and engineer, electrical and refrigeration officers together. The chief steward/purser, named Mortimer, an old timer on the ship, like the captain and chief engineer, had his own little coterie. I was blissfully ignorant of these social distinctions.

The second day at sea the captain sent for me and asked me the number of my certificate, which he said was not in the articles, the legal document which each member of the crew signs as a contract recording salary levels, food and living conditions, behaviour, and the like. It is vital as an indication of the standards below which seamen and shipping companies must not fall.

I replied brightly, "I have not passed my certification yet." "My God! They've sent me a bloody impostor! Never before have I had an officer without a master's ticket. Now I have to put up with a 'makey learny'. Go below to your cabin. You will not be allowed to take charge of a watch. You'll go on the four to eight a.m. watch with the chief officer."

I was secretly pleased about this arrangement. I

knew I was green. I'd not been on a ship for years, and never in charge of a watch. I liked the chief officer very much, and my friends Dalgleish and Galbraith were quartermasters of that watch. At 4 a.m. next morning I went up to relieve the second officer, expecting to find the chief officer. But the chief officer had not done watch keeping for some years and no one had told him that he was supposed to be on watch with me. So I kept the dawn watch, helped by my two quartermasters, who were glad to re-learn and practise the arts of navigation they had learned as young men, but had not had the chance to use for many years.

The chief officer, or mate, as we called him, came up at seven, having been finally alerted, and asked how I had got on. One of the quartermasters piped up, "You don't need to worry, sir. Mr Foss can do the work perfectly well. We'll call you if he needs help." The mate never came on watch again. A few days later, Dalgleish said to me, "I don't know if I ought to tell you, but the captain told us to keep an eye on you because he says Foss is a German name and you might be a spy. Of course, 'Hopper', the Captain's name, is German, too, so it puts me in a funny position!"

Foss is not a German name, but I felt the captain's remark was undermining my position with men for whom I had a responsibility. I did not like it, and it set me thinking about a number of the 'old man's' actions which seemed to me inappropriate for someone in his position. With little to occupy my mind on the dawn watch, I began making a note of several such flaws, coming up with thirteen. At the end of my watch I went to my cabin and typed up the list and decided it was my responsibility to bring them to the captain's attention. I was so green, so little accustomed to a ship's hierarchy, I assumed he would be grateful to me for being helpful.

I found him walking up and down on his deck, getting some exercise, and asked if I could have a word with him. He looked surprised and asked what about? I handed him the piece of paper to read. He glanced at it and said sharply, "What's this all about?" I was startled by his antagonistic manner, but nervously explained. His face was turning red. He shouted, "Go to your cabin. I'll land you at St Vincent (where we were to take bunker oil) for mutiny."

I was staggered and before heading to my cabin could not resist saying, "I hope you're a wealthy man, captain."

He looked puzzled and asked what I meant.

"Well, if you land me at St Vincent I'll sue you for wrongful dismissal, and that would cost you a lot of money."

"Go to your cabin," he roared.

On my way there I had to pass the chief officer's cabin. His door was open and he called me in and pointed to a ventilator. "That opens on to the captain's deck and I was an unwilling listener to your conversation with him. Before you say a word I want to thank you. You expressed all the things some of us have wanted to say to him for some time, but dared not, as he can affect our promotion if we cross him. I can assure you that everyone on board will appreciate it."

"That's all very well, but what do I do now?"

"Just go on as if nothing had been said to you. It can't make things worse, and it might make things easier."

When it came time for me to go on watch again I went up fifteen minutes early and crept across the captain's deck to relieve the second mate. Then I began my watch, which was very absorbing at that moment because we had entered an area in which we had been warned of submarine attacks and my eyes were glued to binoculars. I had forgotten about the captain, when I sensed someone close by. I stand close to six foot, five inches and I looked down to see him, short and stocky, beside me.

"Here, Mr Foss, look at this cartoon." He held up a magazine with a centre-fold Heath Robinson drawing entitled. "The man who dropped the pot of paint at the Royal Review." The King was coming aboard a battleship as a man up the mast was spilling some paint above his Majesty. The crew were falling over in dismay and the Captain was stamping on his cap. Captain Hopper commented quietly, "Just like modern seamen – no guts, no standards, useless."

"That's not true, sir," I protested. "You have some excellent men on this ship."

"Then why have they never had the guts to tell me what you did this morning?"

"Because you hold their future in your hands. You can't do anything like that to me. I'm lucky to be here and if you sacked me I could always find another job."

"They're all worms," he snorted and walked

away. Then he turned and came back. "Are you any good at accounts?" he asked.

I said I was.

"I don't trust the purser. I think maybe he's fiddling and I want someone to check his figures."

The purser and I had become good friends and I thought he was straight. I asked jokingly, "How much will you pay me?"

"You cheeky monkey!" The captain grinned. "Would five pounds be enough?"

That was good money in those days and I agreed.

For the next few evenings after my watch I went to the captain's cabin and made a cursory examination of the accounts. But it was soon clear to me that Captain Hopper was a very solitary man and seemed to be enjoying some company. It dawned on me how lonely was a captain's job.

2

Troubled waters

In May, nineteen hundred and forty, I set sail for home in a convoy from Freetown, in West Africa. The convoy was large, composed of some fifty ships of all kinds – old cargo ships loaded with iron ore and bauxite from West Africa, oil tankers which had joined us after a tedious journey around the Cape from the Persian Gulf, large Indian and Far East traders, and cargo/passenger liners like ourselves from South America. The speed of the convoy was to be slow, set at six knots.

Ours had been selected as Commodore Ship and after the convoy set sail we waited until a rear admiral came aboard and took charge. Then we caught up with the rest and assumed our station in the middle of the front line of the convoy, which had five lines of ten ships each.

The next few days were uneventful. As fourth officer I was keeping the chief officer's watch, four to eight, morning and evening. This was the watch during which most convoy practice manoeuvres were carried out and signals were passed, so there was plenty to keep me from being bored. Then, as I came on watch on the last day of May we received a radio warning that there were submarines in the area. During my watch that evening a torpedo was sighted approaching the convoy from the starboard directly across our bow. The convoy was zig-zagging and as we were turning to port the torpedo crossed our bow and hit the *Clan Ogilvie*, stationed alongside us. It hit her right in the bow, forward of her collision bulkhead, and although she stopped and took all necessary precautions she was able to proceed with the convoy.

At the end of my watch I was relieved by the third officer and went to my cabin. Thirty minutes later, as I was writing a letter, the ship gave a violent lurch to starboard, accompanied by a loud noise sounding like a giant matchbox being squeezed to bits. I picked myself up off the floor and as I reached the cabin door I saw our eighteen-year-old third radio officer, go racing by, obviously panic-stricken. He was clearly headed for a lifeboat. I was scared myself. I called to him, "David, shouldn't you be going to the radio office?"

"Oh, yes, of course," he panted, and bracing himself, he turned round and started walking quickly back in that direction.

On deck an amazing sight greeted me. As a wartime precaution, when we left Freetown all the lifeboats had been swung out on their davits. When the ship had lurched all those on the starboard side had been ducked under the water and were now full of water. Worse still, oil stored for use in the lamps had spilled and spread on the surface of the water and had been ignited by acetylene flares.

Each lifeboat was slopping fiery water over its side as the ship tossed lazily in the Atlantic rollers.

Fortunately there was room for everyone in the port side boats and they were filled and lowered safely away. Finally the only men left were the captain, chief officer, third engineer, bosun, one sailor, the lamptrimmer – the keeper of the deck stores, and myself. The captain was sixty-three years old and seemed dazed by what was happening to his ship. Larry Evans, the chief officer, a capable and cool man, said to him, "Will you please get down into that lifeboat, sir? I will make sure the ship is clear of people and follow you on a raft."

"No, no," said the captain. "I must be the last to leave the ship."

"Either you get down into that boat, sir, or I'll get the fourth mate and the lamptrimmer to put you there by force." The captain looked at us. "All right, I'll go." And we lowered him into the boat we'd kept waiting for him.

Then we searched the ship to make sure no one was left on board. It seemed that everyone was safely away, although a few had sustained injuries, especially a greaser who had been badly scalded when the torpedo entered the forward boiler room.

The chief officer decided to try to get one of the flooded lifeboats away and two of our men grabbed its ropes and tried to do it. The boat was so heavy it stretched the ropes to the limit and as we wrestled with them we failed to notice that the reel on which the forward rope was wound had broken free from the deck in the explosion.

When the chief officer gave the order to let go

in order to drop the boat on the crest of an ocean roller, the reel fell and jammed a young seaman's leg between the rope and the lowering bollard. The rope ate into his leg and every time the ship rolled the whole weight of the lifeboat pressed on his thigh. The third mate raced into the officers' pantry and came out with a bread knife and I was able to saw the lad free. We then called back a lifeboat and lowered him into it.

We stayed with the ship for another hour in case it could be saved. When we saw that was out of the question we decided to leave. Then we had to wait for the chief officer to change into his best uniform. "I've only just bought it," he said, "and I'm certainly not leaving it behind." Then we released a life raft and floated away to the tune of the chief officer's lusty rendering of "Roll out the barrel".

We were soon picked up by a lifeboat which had already delivered its survivors to the South Wales grain ship *Beignon*, a new vessel which the Vice Commodore had designated as our rescue ship. As soon as we were all aboard, the *Beignon* set sail at speed to catch up the convoy. We all appreciated her stopping to pick us up, because it made her a sitting duck for any lurking submarines. As she got under way we looked across to see our old ship lazily turn over and sink.

The *Beignon* had a crew of some thirty and had now taken aboard more than one hundred survivors. Quarters were crowded; I found myself with seven other young officers sharing the deck of the chief officer's office. Between us we had only two life jackets. That was not the worst; the ship had just two lifeboats, each capable of holding about thirty, and one small "jolly boat", holding maybe six.

Around one thirty that night the door to the office was flung open and the *Beignon's* boatswain called in, "You'd better get yourselves ready; a torpedo has just missed us!" A few minutes later there was a terrific explosion in the fore part of the ship and she began to lurch slowly but surely down by the head. She had one huge hold, designed to carry bulk cargoes like grain; the torpedo had entered this hold and as the grain poured out, the water poured in, and the vessel continued steaming downwards.

We all jumped up. Automatically I put on my shoes, then kicked them off and headed for the deck. As I stepped over the storm step the water was up to my ankles and followed me as I climbed aft. On the way to the boat deck I ran into our doctor, an elderly man who tended to imbibe heavily and was in no condition to face another torpedoing. I grabbed him by the armpits and called for help, but in the dark and amidst the noise no one saw or heard me. The doctor struggled in my arms and he was wet and slippery and slithered out of sight in the water. Then I plunged into the midships accommodation to try to find our two injured seamen, but the water level was now so high I couldn't force the door open. Later I found they had already been rescued.

I ran back on to the deck to find that both lifeboats had already been launched and some fifty fellows were milling around in the dark on a strange ship, with no idea what to do. I took charge of a few men to launch the "jolly boat" successfully and just then the Commodore appeared and asked very quietly, "Is there any room for me in the boat?"

"Certainly, sir," I said, and pointing to some ropes hanging over the ship's side, asked, "Can you slide down one of these?" He was a man over sixty who had retired and returned as Convoy Commodore, and I quickly added, "Go down to the deck below, sir; it's not so far to jump from there."

The Commodore went below and began swinging himself out on a rope which I saw was not long enough to reach the water. So I was able to seize it and lower him hand over hand into the boat. Then I yelled, "Get her away," as the small boat, with already a dozen men aboard was veering about as the rollers swept past.

One of the seamen had followed regulations laid down in the lifeboat certificate and had run the painter (the rope from the bow of the "jolly Boat") forward and made it fast. The *Beignon* was still moving forward and to my horror I noticed that as they paid out this painter it was still made fast in the boat with a splice and no one had a knife with which to cut it. Here was the small boat, full of men, lashed firmly to a sinking ship.

There was nothing I could do; the forward end of the painter was already well under water. I had to stand and watch as the "jolly boat" and its human cargo disappeared beneath the waves.

Then I scrambled to the stern and jumped into the sea and as I rose to the surface grabbed some floating debris. I remember saying a quick prayer

– "OK, God, if you want to take me, I don't mind." Soon afterwards from the top of a large roller I saw nearby one of the lifeboats, its white paint shining in the moonlight. I swam to it and caught hold of a lifeline looped around the boat. Immediately one of the men above me yelled, "Let go; our boat's already over-crowded and one more person will sink us!"

I couldn't help smiling and asked, "May I hang on for a bit and catch my breath?"

Another voice, which I recognised as the carpenter's, called out, "Mr Foss? You better come aboard; there's no officer to take charge," and pulled me up. When someone complained there was no room, "Chippy," a very powerful man, said, "There'd be room if I knocked you overboard."

I looked around; every thwart was packed with men, some sitting on the knees of others. There were half a dozen oars in the water being pulled in different directions. I needed to act. I prayed for strength and wisdom and asked Chippy to pray too. "I don't know how," he said. "Just say to God, 'Please help us, otherwise we'll all be corpses.' "

Then I ordered anyone with an oar not facing my way to throw it out. There was a chorus of protest. I shouted, "I'm in charge. We are some one hundred miles from land – no hope in hell of rowing that distance. Our best way is to stay right here, hope the radio officer sent an SOS before we sank and that some ship is looking for us."

I ordered men with seaboots to take them off

and use them to bail water from the boat to lighten
it.

The eastern sky was just beginning to lighten
when someone in the bow shouted, "Look, there's
a periscope; keep quiet; they might hear us."
Someone added that Germans machine gunned
lifeboats to prevent them giving their position
away. The periscope seemed to remain stationary
and someone suggested it was a submarine charg-
ing its batteries. A great silence fell over the boat.
I prayed as I'd never prayed before, asking God
for direction. He seemed to whisper in my ear,
"It's all right. Go ahead."

As dawn's light grew, we suddenly saw from the
crest of a roller, not a periscope, but the mast of
a destroyer which seemed to be turning away from
us. We gave a great shout, but the ship began
moving away at full speed. Our hope died, but I
ordered the men to continue rowing. About an
hour later, in full daylight, we saw the destroyer
above the rollers once more; she seemed to be
sweeping for a submarine. Those with oars started
paddling furiously and others started paddling
with their hands. Our combined efforts produced
about two knots; then suddenly, from the crest of
a wave we saw her heading our way. Chippy and
I sat in the stern thanking God.

As she pulled alongside and took off our men I
asked for sailors from the destroyer to join me in
a sweep looking for survivors swimming or clinging to wreckage. Before long we had picked up a
boatload, and others went searching. Between us
we picked up most of the crews of the two sunken
ships.

I went up to see the captain of the destroyer. His first remark was, "Do you believe in miracles? I do now. I had received radio orders to rescue a ship that had been torpedoed some fifty miles away and we were on our way when the gunner's mate on the poop rang through to say he thought he'd seen a submarine on the surface. I had to make up my mind what to do and chose to go after what we thought was a sub. It was you."

I said, "Thank you and praise God."

After searching in vain for more survivors the destroyer headed for the UK. The ship was so low on fuel that we sailed at half speed and by the time we sighted the English coast stokers were in the fuel tank brushing out the last of the oil to keep the ship moving. Finally, a great cry of relief went up when a tug from Plymouth appeared to tow us into safety. I was sitting in the stern saying a quiet prayer of thanks and when I stopped, several of the survivors joined in with "Amens". Word had been going around that it was prayer that had saved them.

Arriving in port with only our torn wet clothes, we were taken to a local hotel. As we went in, guests walked out muttering, "What are they doing, letting scruffs like these into our hotel?" We scruffs could not have cared less. We borrowed money to phone home. By the time my turn came to phone it was past two o'clock. Nancy was awoken and asked: "What on earth are you phoning at this time of night?" But when I told her why, she understood.

Then I got some torpedo leave.

My next ship was the *Tacoma Star*, twenty-six

years old, built in the First World War as a fast
meat carrier. She still did sixteen knots and her
refrigeration equipment was very efficient. She had
twin quadruple expansion engines, (for those
interested in technicalities) with Baur Watch
exhaust turbines, she burned coal.

I joined her in Liverpool. She was due to sail
"light ship" – without cargo – for China. In the
engine room she had West Africans; this was my
first time to live and work with them. Soon after
sailing we learned that we were to be the Commodore Ship of a convoy of some two dozen ships
which the *Tacoma Star* was to join off Belfast
Loch. On board was the Convoy Commodore, a
retired admiral.

When the convoy was made up, after much
manoeuvring, our ship was in the middle of the
front row in a formation of eight ships abreast in
three columns. We had hardly turned west to sail
north of Ireland into the Atlantic when thick fog
descended on us, more than twenty ships wallowing along at six knots, close on top of each other,
unable to communicate except by blowing our
identification number on our fog horns – short
range radio still lay in the future. So there was an
incessant din, but nothing to be seen but the swirl-
ing fog.

We were streaming a fog buoy, a Heath Robinson contraption tied on a long line from our stern,
which scooped water up into a fountain by which
the ship astern could keep position. This slow,
noisy, frightening procession went on for hours. I
was glad that as fourth mate I had only to stand,
shaking with fear, and do what I was told. The

captain and admiral were on the bridge the whole
time. The captain was a colourful character known
to us all as "Raider", because whenever a ship was
sighted he would shout, "There's a German raider;
alter course away from her and get extra speed."

During my watch we suddenly heard a colossal
crash, clearly the sound of two ships colliding,
rather than the crunch of a torpedo exploding – a
noise with which I was now very familiar. The
sound of the crash came from directly ahead of us;
there were ships on each side of us, so all we could
do was plod along, keep alert and hope for the
best. One of our radio officers, Sparks, came racing
on to the bridge to say that the *Jersey City*, the
ship that should have been abeam of us on the
starboard side, had collided with a ferry boat crossing from Ireland. He'd heard the SOS from the
ferry – they were sinking.

Immediately afterwards, two ships, locked
together, suddenly loomed out of the fog some fifty
yards directly ahead of us. The chief officer rang
full speed astern both engines, to take the way off
our ship, but with insufficient time to stop us. Very
slowly we pushed between the two ships, the *Jersey
City* and the *Lairds Castle*, forcing them apart as
we moved on, with only scratches to our paint
work. Then we watched the *Jersey City*, now free,
start full speed ahead, rushing off into the fog
ahead of the convoy.

We put our ship back into convoy speed, since
we had to stay clear of the ships astern of us,
although we were all sick with worry about what
might have happened to the *Lairds Castle* crew.
Then Sparks ran on to the bridge again to say that

the *Lairds Castle* was sinking fast and the crew
were taking to the boats.

Just then a loud shout come from our forecastle-
head, "Ship right ahead!" We saw the bow of a
ship coming straight for us. The chief officer
reacted immediately – "Hard to starboard!" Then,
"Midships!" and then "Hard to port!" Our bow
swung clear of the other ship, missing by a few
feet. As we swung back on the opposite course to
her she passed so close alongside us that she broke
our wooden sounding boom, which stuck out
about six feet.

We saw that she was the *Jersey City* and as our
bridge passed hers her captain yelled, "I'm going
back to see if I can rescue the *Lairds Castle* crew!"

Our captain "Raider" said nothing, just kept on
gripping the "dodger", the windbreak, and the
admiral also stood looking quietly ahead as though
all this was just a daily occurrence. For the next
hour none of us on the bridge spoke. For myself,
I just shivered from cold and relaxed fear. I had
thought, how crazy it would be to survive two
torpedoings and then be sunk in a collision. Now
I was quietly thanking God.

Next morning the fog lifted and we slowly made
our way to mid-Atlantic. We never saw the *Jersey
City* again, nor did we hear the fate of the crew
of the *Lairds Castle*. We settled into our routine;
I was on the four to eight watch each morning and
evening and every morning about six thirty the
admiral's yeoman of signals arrived on the bridge.
Five minutes later the admiral arrived to see how
his "chickens" were doing. His first question was
often, "How is the *Cesspool* doing this morning?"

The *Sedgepool* was the slowest ship in the convoy
and had difficulty keeping up with us. I came to
know the old boy well; each evening I was included
in a bridge game with him, his telegraphist and
yeoman. Each morning he told a new joke; one of
his best was about his brother, an infantry subaltern in World War I.

His brother's regiment was engaged with the
Italians, our allies, in holding off the Germans in
a very bloody battle which the allies had won.
Next morning his commanding officer received a
message from the Crown Prince of Montenegro,
whose small army was fighting alongside the allies.
The Prince wished to make three awards to the
most deserving of the British for their valour – the
First, Second and Third Class of the Order of the
Black Mountain, and would the commanding
officer please select three men to receive the decor-
ations? The CO asked his adjutant, "Who the hell
do we recommend?"

The adjutant answered, "As CO, you must
receive the First Class."

"And you should have the Second Class, adjutant. Who in thunder should get the Third?"

"What about giving it to the first man who
passes that window over there?" suggested the
adjutant with a grin. The CO laughingly agreed.

The first man to pass the window was the
admiral's brother, the young subaltern. He was
called in and solemnly informed that he had been
chosen to receive the Third Class Order of the
Black Mountain for his bravery in the recent
action. He was nineteen, very shy and overcome
at the honour.

The troops were lined up for the visit of the Crown Prince, who arrived in a splendid uniform. The CO stepped forward and a medal was pinned on his chest. The adjutant had a larger medal, suspended on a gorgeous ribbon, hung around his neck. When the subaltern's turn came, the Prince embraced him and kissed him on both cheeks, put a vivid sash around his shoulders, pinned a diamond star on his chest and presented him with a scroll proclaiming him a Duke of Montenegro, with a small salary for life. The Third Order had turned out to be the highest honour!

Another of his reminiscences: When he commanded *HMS Renown*, Prince George, later to succeed to the throne, served under him as a midshipman. His mother, Queen Mary, lectured the admiral because when the prince came home there were holes in his socks and underwear. King George, however, told him to "give the little. . . . hell; it's the only time in his life when he'll understand what it is not to be a prince."

The admiral and I became close friends. I learned much from him and enjoyed his fund of stories and wise outlook on life, and it was a sad day for me when we had to land him in Gibraltar and proceed on our way around the Cape for China.

At long last we steamed into Shanghai – what a place! As we made our way up the Whang Po, on which the city lies, we were surrounded by sampans, small boats with flimsy roofs, tied up twenty abreast along the river banks. They were floating towns, with families living in an area of maybe twenty feet long and three feet wide – born, bred, lived and died there on the water. Yet they seemed a happy lot, always laughing and talking and running around.

We tied up to buoys at the Fish Steps, a wide stairway running down the river bank, and soon our ship was crowded with a cheerful gang of porters carrying aboard frozen eggs. In those days the chicken were raised up country and driven several hundred miles to Shanghai, accompanied by small boys who collected their eggs as they were laid and hauled them in sledges into the city. The chickens were killed and dressed for market; the eggs were cracked and run into five gallon cans, deep frozen and held to await a ship's arrival. Then they were shipped to England and around the world.

Along with the porters came a tailor and two shoe makers. They made suits and shoes to measure while you waited – good quality and good workmanship. Ever since I've wondered why British tailors and shoe makers took so long.

One evening the second mate, Freddy Grist, a close friend, together with the chief steward, our seventeen-year-old third radio officer named Lightbody and I clambered into a sampan and were taken to the Fish Steps. We each climbed into a rickshaw, headed for a night out in the International Settlement. We had heard of its night life and wanted to see if the rumours were true. The rickshaw men pulling the second mate and steward began to run ahead of me, and Lightbody was trailing far behind. I became worried about losing him in the Chinese quarter, where the Japanese were the occupying authorities and took little interest in any crime that did not affect their con-

trol. My rickshaw puller took no notice of my calls
to slow down.

As I looked back I saw Lightbody's rickshaw
suddenly veer into a crowded alleyway and disappear. I thought, "My God! They could kill
Sparky for his money, and no one would be the
wiser." I could not stop my rickshaw man until we
were held up at the entrance to the International
Settlement and I shot into the Grand Astor Hotel
to reach a telephone and call the Mission to
Seamen to seek their help. I rushed through the
revolving door into the hotel lobby, to be faced
by two Japanese soldiers with fixed bayonets. I
revolved out through the doors faster than I'd
come in. We were not yet at war with Japan, but
the atmosphere between our two countries had
become very tense.

With my two friends I hurried to the Seaman's
Mission, but the padre there could only suggest
phoning the Japanese police. When I did so, they
replied that one of their policemen had been mur-
dered and all their force was busy trying to find the
murderer. So we sat around and played snooker all
evening, hoping for news of Sparky. Finally we
hired a taxi to take us to the ship. Before rushing
to tell the captain about Sparky I decided to look
in to his cabin. There he was, fast asleep. I woke
him to find out what had happened; his rickshaw
man, having taken him a mile from the International Settlement, dropped the shafts and
demanded ten dollars to take him there. Sparky, a
Scot, offered fifty cents and was refused.

So Sparky decided to walk back, hoping to find
the way. The rickshaw man followed, shouting

and collecting a hostile crowd. He eventually came on a Japanese policeman, but when Sparky asked the way he grinned, cleared his throat and spat into Sparky's face, to the delight of the crowd. He hurried on and encountered a huge, bearded, turbaned Indian Sikh soldier, one of the force that policed the International Settlement. Sparky rushed over to him and asked the way. The Sikh looked him over, placed his hand on Sparky's behind and said, "I'll give you five dollars to sleep with me tonight, pretty boy."

Sparky, now thoroughly scared, pushed through the crowd down a side street that he thought might lead back to the Fish Steps. Suddenly he heard a voice shout in English, "Come along, my yellow beauty, you're coming with us." Sparky saw a huge black man emerge from a doorway – Frank, a West African, one of the donkeymen who looked after some of the smaller machinery in our ship's engine room. Frank bellowed to him, offering a woman he'd picked up. Sparky declined, but gratefully accompanied Frank in rickshaws summoned by Frank, and followed by two more rickshaws carrying his girlfriend and parcels. On arrival at the Fish Steps, Frank ordered the girl to load his parcels on to a sampan, put Sparky in, kissed his girlfriend goodbye and threw a handful of coins among the inevitable crowd of Chinese, bellowing them a "Happy Christmas!" Sparky boarded our ship, a subdued and wiser man.

From Shanghai we steamed up the coast to Tsingtao, arriving on a beautiful winter day, but our signals to the port and the pilot boat received no response. For three days we remained at anchor some three miles from port; each time we communicated with our agents and with the port authorities they could only tell us we must wait for the Japanese to make up their minds. Finally, a tug boat came out with a Japanese doctor who said, "So sorry, we didn't notice you." Each day a health officer had come out with a pilot to ships a few hundred yards away and they had been escorted into port.

The doctor ordered all the crew on deck for a health check, lined up in seniority of rank, with the captain in the front. He checked off every name on the crew list, then ordered everyone to lower their trousers and underpants and called the captain to stand before him. The captain assumed what dignity he could, all of us knowing that the exercise was intended to humiliate us. Our African crew members protested loudly, calling him an evil little man. But we submitted to his orders, knowing well that with war raging in Europe and likely to break out in the East we could not be too careful.

Relieved to tie up in port, we found Tsingtao a clean and pleasant town. It had been a German possession for many years, until recently the Germans had departed and the Japanese had taken over. From there we sailed as far north as Chinwangtao, where I was amazed to see dock labourers walking a hundred yards down the quay with four hundred and fifty-pound cases of dried eggs on their backs, then up a gangway to the ship, where the cases were lowered into a hold. Then we returned to Shanghai to complete our loading before sailing for home. The ordinary men and women of China had made a deep impression on me, with their cheerfulness, full of laughter, jokes and singing, despite their gruelling hard work.

As we sailed south, approaching the channel between Taiwan, then known as Formosa, and mainland China the seas became increasingly rough and over the radio we received warning of a typhoon. It hit us midway through the Formosa Straits. Never had I seen such seas. I stood on the bridge and looked ahead at the tips of the huge waves above the top of our foremast. One wave crashed down on the foredeck and swept away the windlass – the heavy engine used for hoisting in the anchors to the forecastle head into the cable locker. It broke all our lifeboats to pieces, tore away the funnel and flooded the engine room to a depth of twenty-six feet. The ship broached round to lie broadside on, rolling more than forty-five degrees each way as she rose sideways over the huge rollers, some of them more than one hundred feet high.

From this experience I stored away in my mind a safety lesson which was to stand me in good stead years later: a ship is often safer in such huge seas wallowing broadside on to the waves. Although it is very uncomfortable, she rides great rollers better and more safely that way.

The storm blew this way for a few days, then we sailed through the calm centre, and then out again into its full force. During this last battering I went on watch at four a.m., short of sleep from the water's frenzy. One idea was racing around in my mind, and crazy as it was, I couldn't resist passing it on to Captain "Raider", who was still on bridge, looking haggard and close to exhaustion.

"Sir," I said, "what do you think would happen if I had the courage to hold out my hand and say, 'Peace, be still' to the storm? Do you think the sea would calm?" He stared hard at me, then he said, "I'm going down below for a bit." It was the first time he had left the bridge for two or three days. I heard later that he had gone straight to the chief officer's cabin and told him what I'd said. The chief, like the rest of us, was tired out, but they had a good laugh together, then he said, "That's the most sensible thing I've heard in a long time." And they both went to their beds and slept.

When the storm did eventually move away we had to tackle the job of reaching Singapore in our crippled condition. Luckily we had a small petrol-driven pump in our deck house and with this we started pumping out the engine room until we could light boilers and get the steam pump operating. Eventually, after rigging a false funnel, we were able to steam slowly to Singapore, where we spent several weeks making repairs.

The long trek from Singapore to Capetown was uneventful and we spent only twenty-four hours in Capetown before making our way back to Liverpool. There was one incident in Capetown which proved noteworthy. Just as we were about to sail a lorry arrived alongside us and men threw two long and heavy boxes on board, shouting, "This is your anti-aircraft equipment. Instructions are in the box," and drove off.

We already had one five-inch gun aboard, made in nineteen hundred and eleven, but still in working condition. I had been designated gunnery officer and had trained a gun crew of Africans to fire it. That had not been easy. They went through the drill very well, slick and efficient, until the day we fired a practice round with a live shell. They had never seen or heard a gun fired before, and no one had told them it produced a loud bang. So when it was fired, they all raced for shelter, thinking something had gone wrong. It took several days to get them back to fire the gun again.

When we unpacked the anti-aircraft gun thrown aboard in Capetown I found it was a machine gun, made in France by Hotchkiss, and had to be assembled. Fortunately I had an old three badger naval rating, called back from retirement, who had taught us how to handle the five-incher. He and I studied the instruction manual, printed in French, and somehow managed to assemble it. The bullets were held in a long canvas belt, and someone had to stand by and stuff the bullets in as the gun was fired.

The engineers made a mounting for the gun and the great day came when we aimed it at the sky and fired. It fired one bullet and jammed. We stripped it down, re-read the instructions and re-assembled it. We fired one more bullet and it jammed. That was the best we ever did with it. On our arrival in Liverpool an armament officer looked it over; "These guns were designed for the Sahara desert," he said, "to be borne on a camel. In moist air the belt shrinks and the gun jams." And he went off with it. Later, I heard that some of our clever people had bought one thousand of them from the French for anti-aircraft defence for the Merchant Marine.

We all felt proud of ourselves as we docked in

Liverpool. We had delivered several thousand tons of badly needed foodstuffs to our beleaguered country. We lay in Gladstone Dock and slowly discharged our cargo. My wife Nancy came to be with me. She stayed at the Oriel Hotel in Bootle, a good old pub not far from the docks. One afternoon she reached the docks with an armful of cakes and goodies, to find a long line of railway trucks blocking the way. As she stood there, a dock policeman came over and said, "It's not going to move; why don't you duck under the buffers and climb through?" As she did so, the train began to move. The policeman dived and pulled her out. Nancy reached the ship, to find it listed over towards the dock and had to climb a rope ladder that was hanging free. Wobbling through the air, clutching the precious cakes, she managed to reach the deck.

I was not on duty that evening and returned with her to the hotel. That night saw the start of eight nights of bombing of the docks, and during the course of the raid a German bomb fell on the Customs House, much to the glee of our sailors, who cordially distrust Customs on principle. Nancy and I headed for the hotel cellar, but found it too crowded; it also housed big boilers and seemed to us more dangerous than our bedroom, so we went back there to sleep. Then a bomb landed close by and blew our bay window right across the bed, with us in it. Almost immediately the all clear was sounded. We sat up, looked at one another and laughed ourselves silly, thankful that it had not been worse.

I decided I must go down to the ship to see how

she had fared. In the middle of town I found almost
every house on fire. I ran into one of the laziest
dockers working on our ship, going from house to
house fighting the flames. No wonder, I said to my
self, he looks so lazy by day if he's fighting fires at
night. When I tried to cross Millers Bridge a man
stopped me and said it was down, there was no
way to cross. So I said I would cross by the railway
lines. "Don't you dare," he said. "You can't; I
know; I'm the mayor."

Eventually I managed to reach the dock gates
and found them guarded by soldiers. When they
tried to stop me, saying that there were unexploded
bombs in the docks, I told them I had to reach my
ship and went on through. I found her sitting on
the bottom, the main deck eighteen inches above
the surface. The exhausted third officer told me
what had happened. He had been on the dock
when a bomb dropped through the boat deck,
through the pillow of the second officer (who was
not aboard), hit the starboard engine and blew it
through the side of the ship, which promptly sank.
Sadly, another bomb had hit the huge store into
which we had moved most of the frozen eggs,
gutting it and spoiling our precious cargo, as our
noses told us only too well during the next few
days.

When I sent the third officer off to get some rest
he told me he had sent Irons, the bosun, to the
Oriel Hotel to fetch me. We must have passed each
other in the rubble on the docks. He told me later
that he had knocked on the bedroom door and,
when Nancy said come in, he had looked at her
lying on the bed with the remains of the bay

window around her and black with dust from the damaged walls. Both had roared with laughter.

I went through the ship looking for casualties. There was only one, an elderly donkeyman, who had been resting when he was hit by British anti-aircraft shrapnel which had penetrated three steel bulkheads and killed him instantly. My first priority then was to get to a telephone to try to reach company engineers and salvage men – anyone who could get to work on the ship. Most telephones were out of order and I set off on the dock to find one that worked. I also went in search of food for breakfast for those on board.

On the road I ran into the company's engineer superintendent. In our company superintendents were treated as gods. I did not share that attitude, especially that morning, as I thought of his having enjoyed a nice quiet sleep on the outskirts of town.

"How's the *Tacoma*?" he asked.

"Fine," I said, "she can't sink any more; she's sitting on the bottom."

"My God! Is she badly damaged?"

"Oh, not bad. She's only blown the starboard engine into the dock."

"Oh dear, we'd better hurry back and see what we can do to get her up."

I grinned. "You do that. I'm going to find some breakfast for those of us who didn't have a nice sleep at home."

Later that day I managed to get away and take Nancy over for a rest at a beautiful country home belonging to friends. Then I was back on the *Tacoma* for the night. Although sitting on the bottom, she was still vulnerable to fire bombs. We had seventy tons of wood, which we'd used to pack the refrigerated cargo, now lying on the deck. Sure enough, that night, the Jerries hit us with two "Molotov breadbaskets" – explosive bombs with clusters of incendiaries. They set fire to the stacks of wood. Because our fire pumps were all below the surface we had to tackle the flames with stirrup pumps and buckets lowered into the water.

A sixteen-year-old deck boy did more than anyone to save the ship that night. Somewhere he'd picked up a "tin hat" and ran around the deck spotting incendiary bombs; if he found one unexploded, he'd give it a smart kick over the side. If the bomb had started to burn, he'd scoop it up in his tin hat and throw it into the water. Tragedy struck two nights later. All our crew stayed on board, except for the lad. He was making his way to the large air raid shelter close to our ship, when a bomb hit the shelter, killing everyone in it, and our deck boy.

On another night, with its usual raid, the Dutch ship lying along side us copped a Molotov breadbasket. Most of her crew were off in a nearby air raid shelter, so our crew dashed on board to deal with the fire. While they were fighting the flames a naval patrol came aboard the *Tacoma* and, finding all was well, left. Their officer put in a report praising the Dutch crew and criticising me as duty officer because our ship was deserted!

3

Perilous voyage

When I joined my next ship, the *Melbourne Star*, at Birkenhead I was told that she was loading for an unknown destination – a sure sign in wartime that this would be a dangerous voyage. She was a beautiful ship, twin screw, twenty-knot, thirteen thousand-ton refrigerator liner, with twelve passenger berths. I felt proud to be appointed to her as fourth mate, although I had now obtained my second mate's certificate.

The loading was well under way when delayed action bombs were dropped in our dock. We were not hit, but the authorities decided that we might be in danger from acoustic bombs beneath us, ready to be exploited by the sound of a ship's engines, so we must be moved. As we could use neither tugs nor our own engines, ropes were passed across the dock by rowing boat and then our ship was warped across. Soon after we reached the other side one of the bombs exploded, taking with it our rudder and damaging our hull. So all our cargo had to be discharged and our ship towed across the River Mersey to Herculean Dock, sheltered below the cliff face.

Repairs seemed to take for ever, but at least I was able to get to know our officers and men well. The master, Captain David MacFarlane, was a remarkable man who was later decorated for his services. A New Zealander, small, quiet and neat, he won my total loyalty. Whenever I did anything wrong he never berated me, but I would find a note in my cabin pointing out how I could do better and encouraging me to be my best. The chief officer was a delightful rogue with a great sense of humour. For example, one evening he and I were sitting in a pub, looking down at the *Melbourne Star*, a beautiful sight, in the dry dock. A man was talking with the barman about our ship's great virtues and we heard him bragging that he was her chief officer. I was about to cut him down to size, but my friend stopped me and had a great time drawing the fellow out about his phoney exploits.

Our repairs at last completed, we sailed for Glasgow to load for our secret destination. I was all the more sure our voyage would be dangerous since the company went to great pains to give everyone plenty of leave. But the loading itself proved to be an adventure for me. Among our cargo was a quantity of whisky, which was placed in a special locker, marked as NAAFI stores and guarded by a shore watchman, who was guarded by a military policeman, who was watched by another military policeman, who was himself under the eyes of a plain clothes sergeant. The ship's duty officer was supposed to watch them all.

I was on duty early one morning as the ship's night gang of stevedores were leaving. Some of them were red hot Communists with whom I got on very well; they were the best workers in the gang. As he walked past me, one of them, a shop steward, suggested I look into the case on which the shore watchman was sitting; then he grinned and handed me a copy of the *Daily Worker*. I went straight down the hatch and asked the watchman to stand up. He was annoyed, but I insisted. What was supposed to be a full case of whisky seemed extremely light. I turned it over and found it had been opened and every bottle was gone. Then I noticed that behind the case a tunnel had been opened through the stack of whisky cases. The night gang of dockworkers had already left, delighted no doubt at their devilment as well as their free drinks. The shipping company would have to pay for the missing bottles.

The following weekend I was duty officer, left in charge of loading. We were "battle loading" – which meant that certain goods must be unloaded at top speed. These, therefore, must be loaded last so that they were immediately accessible. I noted that we had already loaded three hundred tons of dynamite, five hundred tons of torpedoes and some three thousand tons of high octane petrol. Then, as I was reading the pre-stowage plan, something looked wrong to me.

I began doing some calculations and became convinced that if we loaded according to these War Office plans the ship would be down at the head and go ever lower as we burned the oil in our bunkers, until she became unsteerable. That would be bad enough under any conditions, but by now I was convinced we were bound for Malta – I had noticed cases in our cargo marked "Malta", with the name inadequately painted out. The island of Malta lay in waters controlled by the enemy and nothing could be worse than operating there with a poorly manoeuvrable ship.

I made up my mind, went up on deck, stopped the loading and sent the labour home. Within minutes a stevedore manager hurried on deck, followed by the Sea Transport Officer – the naval representative on the docks – demanding to know why I'd stopped the work. The stevedore doubted if I was right; the officer said he would report me to the naval authorities and I would be in serious trouble. He added that if our ship was delayed, we would hold up the entire convoy, and the ships waiting at sea to join our convoy would be sitting targets for submarines. I didn't sleep too well that night.

I was having a lie-in around nine-o'clock next morning, since nothing could be done about the loading during the weekend, when the quartermaster came to my cabin. "Sir, there's a bloomin' admiral and all his staff on the gangway and he wants your permission to come aboard."

I jumped out of bed, saying, "Hold him for five minutes while I dress; then bring him along."

In five minutes the admiral, followed by a commander and a lieutenant, came into the cabin.

"May I sit down, please?" said the admiral, smiling.

I showed him to the one chair and sat on my bunk.

"I understand that you have taken upon yourself the grave responsibility of stopping all work and sending the workers away. May I enquire why?"

"Certainly, sir. Because in my opinion the loading plan sent in by the War Office, if adhered to, would make the ship unseaworthy."

The admiral asked pleasantly if I would show him what had made me come to that conclusion.

"Very easily," I replied, and showed him the plans and figures and the calculations I had made and my deductions. "Very interesting, but I'm afraid I don't understand any of it. I'm basically a gunner myself, but you sound as if you know what you're talking about. I will back you on your decision. Good morning, and thank you for your courtesy." He gave me his hand and left.

I ran through my figures three or four times and always came out with the same answers. I slept better the next night, but still not too well. At six-thirty Monday morning there was a knock on my door and an Army man in battle dress charged in.

"I am Major Warren, from the War Office. Why did you stop the loading?"

Wearily I explained once more and waited a little nervously for the explosion.

He exploded, but not in the way I was expecting. "I wonder what idiot made this pre-loading plan. Of course you are right. Let's get to work and replan the loading and make the ship safe."

Major Warren was first class; he knew all there was to know about loading ships. As soon as we had finished I passed the new plan to the stevedores and they began the re-loading. Then we had break-fast together. I asked how he knew so much about

loading refrigerated cargo liners. He laughed and
said it was his job. "Until three weeks ago I was
cargo superintendent for the New Zealand Shipping Line."

When the chief officer came on board the major
told him the whole story, adding "It's on such
small things as this that victory or defeat sometimes hang."

Soon after sailing we received a coded message
confirming that we were bound for Malta, which
at that time was isolated in the enemy controlled
Mediterranean. It held the key to the battles raging
in North Africa. Whether Rommel would succeed
in forcing his way to Egypt depended in large
degree on whether he could maintain his supply
lines across the sea from Italy. Malta was the thorn
in his flesh, an airbase from which his ships were
vulnerable. I had a particular interest in Malta.
My brother Pat, until a few weeks earlier, had
commanded the Wellington bomber squadron
which harassed enemy shipping.

The enemy had prevented all but a handful of
British ships from re-supplying Malta and we knew
that our convoy of fast refrigerated carriers was
eagerly awaited. Our cargoes were so distributed
that even if only a few of our ships got through,
they would bring urgently needed supplies. With
the *Melbourne*'s cargo of high octane fuel, dynamite, submarine torpedoes and warheads, we felt
we were sitting on one big bomb. No one showed
outward fear, but there was a tenseness and a great
deal of nervous joking. I recall a seaman, coming
on the bridge for his watch, asking the chief officer,
"Are we going to be issued with parachutes?"

The trip as far as Gibraltar had been simple, with a few alarms, a lot of gun practice, and some tightening of discipline among a contingent of Royal Artillery men being sent to relieve others in Malta. These men had never been to sea before, nor had they been trained in the use of the Bofors anti-aircraft guns which we had mounted around the ship and which were to be landed on arrival at Malta. In addition, we had on board some cases of Bren guns, which were new to the Army.

I had been delegated the ship's gunnery officer and I, too, knew nothing about Bren guns. Fortunately we had aboard a senior petty officer gunner who was familiar with them, so each day I had him running classes, first for senior NCO's, who then instructed their men who would have to use the Bren guns to protect themselves and their Bofors guns from low flying aircraft.

As we slowly entered the Mediterranean a destroyer steamed out from Gibraltar and fired a line across to us with orders detailing the pattern our convoy was to assume. *Melbourne Star* was to lead the starboard line, with our captain acting as commodore of the convoy, with the help of Admiral Sarel, who would join us with his signal-men and telegraphists. The next two days were passed in manoeuvering our convoy into position for the next crucial stage of our voyage.

There were six armed transports, our sister ship, the *Sydney Star* and the New Zealand Shipping Company's *Durham*, the Blue Funnel's *Deucalion*, the *Port Chalmers* and a Wilhelmson's of Norway ship. Our main escort was composed of three Tribal class destroyers headed by the *Cossack*, three F class, and the cruiser *Edinburgh*. With us also went a small task force with the aircraft carrier *Ark Royal*, the cruiser *Manchester* and their escorting destroyers.

With so many ships in close proximity the work-up manoeuvres were essential for establishing control over the area which each ship covered with her guns, so that no one killed people on our own ships. We worked hard from dawn to dusk until we became part of what was later known as the great "H Force" under the command of Admiral Somerville. All day signals flew from his masthead in naval code, but just before dusk a completely new set of flags were unfurled. It took us a few minutes to realize they were using the international code used by all merchant seamen. The signal read "Time for supper."

On the third day we moved off together for Malta in lovely calm weather that began to lull us into the belief our voyage would be peaceful. At four a.m. I relieved Mike Tallack, the second officer on the bridge. No ships were showing any lights and all that could be seen was the phosphorescence of the water at their bows and in their wakes. But Mike was worried. "I haven't seen anything of the *Sydney Star* for more than an hour." I walked over with him to the starboard wing to look aft. No sign of her. She was never seen again.

We were immediately distracted by something else – a line of phosphorescence headed directly toward us from starboard. "Do you think that's a torpedo?" asked Mike urgently. I answered hopefully, "No, I think it's dolphin." But it didn't alter course as would a dolphin as it came close. It came right at us. We held our breath, waiting for the explosion. There was none. We rushed to the port side and saw the phosphorescent line appear there, then disappear between the *Port Chalmers* and the *Durham*. If it had been a torpedo, it was set too deep and had gone under us.

My feelings of relief were shattered at dawn, when a lookout shouted, "Aircraft approaching on the starboard bow." Then another lookout yelled, "Aircraft approaching from the port quarter." There were more shouts. Aircraft were all around us, coming in at about ten thousand feet. The cruiser began firing its heavy AA guns and fighters started taking off from the *Ark Royal*.

As the attacking planes headed over us we could see their bomb bay doors open and clusters of bombs falling. At the same time, Stukas, the dreaded dive bombers were headed at us. A lookout suddenly reported aircraft coming very low on our port side, obviously torpedo planes. Our raw soldiers manning the guns were looking very trigger happy and it was my task to make sure they didn't open fire until the planes were within range, so I stood on top of the "monkey island", a deck above the wheelhouse, alongside Admiral Sarel, and kept sending a message over the 'phone forward and aft, "Hold your fire."

Fortunately high bombing of ships is inaccurate and not one bomb hit any of the twenty ships of our group. There seemed to be few dive bombers and only the *Manchester* and perhaps the *Ark Royal* seemed to receive a hit. The H Force pulled off to the north to try to draw Kesselring's "air circus" away from the transports. Meantime we were too busy dealing with the Italian torpedo bombers to notice much else. The whole attack lasted only about five minutes before all the aircraft were headed back to Sicily, no doubt to reload.

I walked round our gun points to see if anyone was hurt. Everyone was all right. When I went aft, the gunner in charge of the heavy AA gun, Petty Officer Spicer, the only professional gunner among us, came over to me and shook my hand. "Well done, sir, first class." I was staggered, had no idea what he was talking about; "What did I do so well?" "Standing up there, sir, with all those machine gun bullets flying about, keeping our men's guns from opening up too soon."

What machine gun bullets? I hadn't seen or heard any. I hurried back to my post on "monkey island" and was shocked to see bullet holes on the plastic armour, which only reached waist high. I sat down, feeling sick.

I hadn't been brave; I hadn't realised the danger; I'd acted idiotically. I knew another attack would be coming soon and was scared at the thought of standing up there again. For a few minutes I sat there praying. I needed God or some power beyond myself that day. I was shaking with fright. But when the planes returned, it was not as difficult as I'd expected.

That night we passed close to Pantaleria, a small Italian island where we knew motor torpedo boats were based. We had heard that they had long range, heavy calibre guns. Those big guns scared me more than any other weapons. In the darkness we heard the engines of the MTB's moving around to the south and to the west of us. Suddenly the heavens were lit up by a "snowflake" rocket and bright lights drifted down above us, illuminating the whole convoy. But, strangely, no guns opened up on us.

As we entered Malta's Grand Harbour thousands of people were hanging over the cliffs shouting a welcome to us. What an arrival! We moored at the first pair of buoys just inside the breakwater. Should any attack come from seaward, we would be the first target. That first night was hot, and feeling very tired, I pitched a hammock on the boat deck. As duty officer that night and as gunnery officer, I felt I must be handy in case of an emergency.

I was awakened by a tremendous roar of engines near the ship, ran to the side and saw a large motor boat approaching us at about thirty knots. It passed us a few feet to starboard. I could see no one in it. It was only later next morning I learned how fortunate we had been. The boat was found stranded, packed with explosives. It was one of three which had been launched by a parent Italian ship. Each was fitted with a launchable seat on which a steersman slid into the water after pointing the boat at a target, to be rescued by a motor torpedo boat.

The first boat had sped under the bridge connecting the seawall with the mainland, but had missed every ship in the harbour. The second had struck the pylon in the middle of the bridge, blowing it up and blocking the harbour entrance. The third had missed everything. We were kept awake

the rest of the night by guns trying to sink the
parent ship and its rescue motor boat. But that
was a small price to pay; we were safe and sound.
I had a great deal to be thankful for.

With more time on my hands I went over in
my mind the adventures of the past months – the
torpedoing of the *Avalona Star*, the typhoon in the
Pacific in the *Tacoma Star*, the bombing and sinking in Liverpool, and now the air attack outside
Malta and the attempt to blow us up in its harbour. I had seen people holding steady through it
all. Each seemed to have his own way of maintain-
ing his sanity. Some let go the pressure by drinking,
others by wild partying, womanising. I knew I was
as scared as anyone, but although I enjoyed some
wild celebrations to ease tension, I felt I was fortunate; I had found a different way.

My desperate call on the Almighty of a few
nights before was not an isolated incident. For
some years I had turned to God for courage, but
also for direction. It had begun several years earlier
when I came face to face with the kind of person
I was. It is fashionable nowadays to blame one's
shortcomings on one's early upbringing and my
youthful years were certainly unusual.

My father left home when I was three and it
was not until I was twenty-one that I had a conversation with him. I had taken my wife, whom I had
married when I was nineteen, to London for a few
days. We called on an old friend of both mother
and father, and the only link I had with father.
Hannen Swaffer was at that time one of the best
known journalists on Fleet Street. I rang his door-
bell and "Swaffy" greeted us in his pulpit style

voice and added, "Come in; I have someone I want you to meet." A man I did not recognise joined us. "Here, Bill," said Swaffy, "meet your son Denis and your daughter-in-law Nancy. Oh, by the way, Bill, I forgot to tell you that you are now a grandfather."

It was an emotional occasion, but we were soon joined by others and had little chance to talk. Father invited us to lunch next day at Genaro's, a fashionable restaurant. Father asked us to call him "Bill", which seemed more fitting than "father", and I learned something about his life. He was at that time working as sports editor for the *Sunday Referee*, a newspaper produced by Radio Normandie. As Nancy and I read the menu our mouths were watering and we looked forward to a sumptuous lunch.

An elderly man approached us and Bill greeted him warmly, "Good day to you, Mr Genaro," and introduced Nancy and me. We shook hands, but he didn't seem very glad to meet us. Then he said to Bill, "Are you having lunch here?"

"Yes, of course."

"And may I ask who is paying?"

"I am, of course," said Bill.

"Then may I see your money in advance, please? You already owe me fifty pounds and I can extend you no more credit."

Father looked very upset and Genaro turned to me; "I am sorry to embarrass you and your wife, but you know how bad your father is with money. We must draw a line somewhere."

All I knew about father's finances was that he must make about ten times what I did. "It's all

right, Mr Genaro," I said. "I'll pay," hoping I had
enough money. Nancy was looking at me in a way
that said – "pick the cheapest thing on the menu."

Despite this uncomfortable start we enjoyed
lunch. Bill was excellent company and I learned
more about his life, which I already knew from
Swaffy was a very colourful one. He had been a
Parliamentary correspondent for the *Morning
Post*, a rugby correspondent for the *Daily Telegraph*; he had produced *Hay Fever* for Noel
Coward at the Haymarket Theatre. He had also
been a very early member of the Fabian Society
and had gone to Spain during the Civil War to
write a book about it. I gathered that he had con-
sorted with H. G. Wells and other Left-wing lib-
erals, but also lived a capitalist life style. I liked
him, and I felt very sorry for him. This was the
last time I ever saw him.

Mother was the daughter of a hotelier in
Bournemouth, an unbending man who reared his
family of five daughters and two sons in a very
stern manner, according to mother. When my
father left mother in nineteen hundred and nineteen to live with a German girl he made no financial provision for mother and their three sons and
a girl named Jane, whom he had casually adopted.
Mother was at her wits' end, she told me later,
and had phoned father's friend, H. G. Wells and
asked if he needed a housekeeper – his house was
always chaotic. She told him over the phone her
desperate plight and he responded by letting her
and her four young children settle into the top
floor of his house. He said, "Rebecca (Rebecca
West, who was living with him) is always too busy

to take care of the shopping and cleaning. You could be very useful."

Before long, grandmother Exton persuaded mother to move away from what she called "an evil influence" and mother's brother Leo gave her a job as manageress of his Linden Hall Hydro in Bournemouth. This job dictated the manner of our upbringing. Mother had to live in the hotel and we children were taken care of by an elderly couple, Captain and Mrs Marples, in a small house in the neighbouring town of Boscombe. They treated us firmly, but kindly. My only friends were my brothers; no playmates came to our house; we attended no church or Sunday school, as mother had a firm hatred of organised religion.

At age five I was sent off to boarding school, where I was made to work hard, but enjoyed the life more than at home, and from there went to the Nautical College at Pangbourne. I think mother hoped that its firm discipline would tame some of my wild mischief at school. It did not. I was for ever in trouble because of some misdemeanour, experienced every form of punishment and graduated without any promotions or distinctions of any kind.

Summer was a difficult time for our family, since mother was very busy with a hotel full of guests, and when I was thirteen she solved the problem by packing my oldest brother Pat and me off on a trip on a collier. We joined the old, rusty vessel, covered with coal dust, and were signed on as ship's boys on her run to Oporto, Portugal. For one shilling per month and our board we chipped paint, trimmed coal, washed dishes, even kept look-out sometimes on the forecastle in the small hours of the morning.

Next year I sailed in a small old freighter to Chantenay on the Loire. In the Bay of Biscay my cabin mate and I were washed out of our bunks by a wave smashing through the porthole. Most of my time was spent peeling potatoes, washing dishes and helping in the galley. I also grew up beyond my years. After a dinner in a French inn the *patronne* and her husband introduced their thirteen-year-old daughter to me as a virgin who would be honoured to sleep with me that night. I was fascinated, but shocked, and amidst the derision of my shipmates declined the offer. It was not long, however, before I succumbed to the sexual enticements I encountered on my travels.

I left the Naval College in nineteen hundred and thirty-two at the age of sixteen and signed on with *TSS Devon* of the New Zealand Shipping Company as a cadet, an apprentice to becoming a merchant ship's officer. It was not an exalted job, but we were in the middle of the Depression, with more than three million unemployed, and I felt fortunate to find work. The *Devon* was a refrigerated cargo ship going "light ship" (without cargo) from Liverpool non-stop to South Australia to load meat. Most of our crew consisted of thirty-nine apprentices like myself. I repeated the Australian trip a second time.

During my next leave I met Nancy. She was staying with her parents in mother's hotel. She was sweet, elfin, and a powerful tennis player. She made a great impression on me. When I rejoined the *Devon* I found it laid up, due to the Depression.

I was kept on as one of five apprentices to assist in the maintenance of five ships berthed together.

One Saturday I went walking through the Cornish countryside with a fellow apprentice. Larking around on a cliff edge, I fell fifty feet or more and finished up in hospital with three fractures in my spine and one in my skull. Lashed immovable in a spinal bed, doctors rated my chances of living as minimal. But I was young and exuberant and fooled them.

When I was able to leave hospital I went to stay with mother in her hotel. There I spotted a very attractive young woman who was visiting with her parents. At the next Saturday evening dance I walked across the floor and asked her for a dance. We got on well and danced together for most of the evening. At half past ten she looked at her watch and said it was time for bed.

"Why so early?" I asked.

"I want to get up early, so I need to go to bed early."

"Tomorrow's Sunday," I objected. "Why get up early?"

"I like to be up by six o'clock every morning."

"Good God, what for?"

"I always spend an hour listening to God," she said quietly.

I mentally took a step back, because she had seemed a charming and balanced girl. She must be a religious maniac. As she left, I called after her, "Ask God if he has any messages for me."

She replied, "I'll certainly do that."

The evening was spoiled for me. I chatted for a while with her parents and they told me their daughter had met up with a religious body at Oxford University known as the Oxford Group. They were very much opposed to it. That made me interested; I was a snob to whom anything to do with Oxford had an appeal; and the parents struck me as a couple of fuddy-duddies with whose ideas I automatically disagreed. I was up unusually early next morning and met the girl coming out of breakfast. I greeted her with, "How was God this morning?"

She said, "He gave me a message for you."

I asked very guardedly what it was.

"God seemed to say it was a pity that a young man like you, with your education and privileges, wastes his life as you do, when you could be doing so much to help the unemployed."

I was flabbergasted and blurted out, "God's got a bloody cheek."

That day she and her parents went home to Leeds, leaving me feeling secretly that her challenge was one that somehow appealed to me. I did nothing about it and was soon enjoying my returning health and strength, but also bored with life. Several months later a nephew of my uncle Leo dropped in on me with a plea for help. Uncle Leo, he said, was pressing him to attend a religious meeting; could I think up a good excuse for not going? I asked him what kind of a meeting. "The Oxford Group."

"Now that's different. They have lovely girls. Why don't we both go?"

"Oh no, they all have prominent teeth and adenoids."

But I persuaded him. We walked into a crowded

hall in which a meeting was already in progress. A genial young man who was leading it saw us and invited us to seats up front. My cousin tried to back out, but I put my newly acquired pipe in my mouth, flipped my scarf round my throat and strode up front with bogus aplomb. I don't recall much about the meeting, but afterwards, still putting on a bold face, I strolled up to the young leader of the meeting and told him I had a few questions. He asked, "Are you genuinely interested, or just curious? If just curious, forget it; I'm busy. But if you really want to know more, come and have tea with me tomorrow. I'm Reg Owbridge, and here's my address."

I left, furious, but mother surprised me by asking about the meeting and next day urged me to visit Reg. Reluctantly I did so. We drove out to a nearby hill top and sat in the car on a chilly March late afternoon, a very unemotional setting. Reg described in very down-to-earth fashion how he had measured his life against absolute moral standards, admitted to himself where he needed to change and asked God's help and direction.

I said I didn't believe in God.

Reg replied that that was no problem. "You're a reasonable chap, so why not try listening to God, just in case he does exist and has a wonderful future for you?"

It ended by his giving me a pencil and paper and we sat quiet for maybe twenty minutes. All I wrote was, "You don't need God to tell you the things you do wrong. You bloody well know." When I read this to Reg, he laughed and suggested I tell him "those dreadful things." So I told him about "knocking off" a masseuse in the hotel, swiping shaving kits and other things from the hotel, using mother's car when she was asleep – and so on.

Reg laughed again and said he'd had the same kinds of thoughts when he had first listened. Then he asked, "So, what are you going to do about them?"

I said I would do nothing. Anything I did would upset my whole life. Reg replied that if I didn't have the guts to give it a try, then let's drive home. His crack about guts upset me. It was true. The outcome was that, feeling a fool, I looked up at the sky, wagged my finger and said, "God, if you exist, which I doubt, I'll give this a go for a fortnight, but if you don't produce a few miracles very quickly, count me out."

My first step was to set things straight with my masseuse friend at the hotel, telling her about the experiment I was making, apologising to her for exploiting her. To my amazement, she broke into tears of relief and told me she had been longing to break off our relationship, scared of my mother and losing her job. We stopped sleeping together and became good friends.

Next I knew I must come clean with mother, but didn't dare to until one day she rounded on me and said, in her fierce style, "For God's sake, get it off your mind, whatever it is; I'm tired of your waffling."

I poured out all the things – nicking from the hotel, using her car and petrol. Like the masseuse, mother dissolved in tears – something I'd never seen before. She told me how happy she was! She'd known about all these things; she had heard me

take the car out at night and had lain in bed scared
that I would drink too much and have an accident.
It was the start of a new relationship; I began to
know and understand and love mother as I had
never done before.

A new spirit entered our whole family, bit by
bit. One morning, when I was in bed with bron-
chitis, my brother Hannen came into my room
with a friend. He'd just come in from an all night
celebration with his dance band, still in his dinner
jacket, with his shirt front decorated with the sig-
natures of all the band, some of whom would
become household names. Hannen demanded to
know what happened to me. Evidently a change
for the better was showing. Talking about it was
the last thing I wanted to do, but he would not be
put off. The result was that Hannen met with my
new friends and he, too, became a different man,
moving from his dance band to devote himself to
a very satisfactory career as a photographer.

Something similar happened soon afterwards to
my older brother Pat, serving as an officer in the
Royal Air Force. He applied a new found faith and
honesty about himself to his responsibilities in the
RAF and had until recently been in charge of the
bomber squadron in beleagured Malta. The trust
and openness he created among his officers and
men kept them going all through the incessant
bombing raids as an effective fighting force.

4

Malta, marriage and mediation

With an average of fourteen air raids a day during our stay in Malta, my experience of being quiet and listening to God for direction and drawing on Him for courage stood me in good stead. The *Melbourne Star* lay tied up to buoys in the middle of Malta's Grand Harbour. A line of barges made fast to one another between the ship and the quay at Floriana provided a simple means to go ashore, but the way was exposed to bombs and anti-aircraft shrapnel.

One day I was visited by a young AC2 from the Air Force whom I had met through friends in the Oxford Group. We were half way along the barges, headed for my ship, when a heavy air raid started. We lay down on our backs on one of the barges as the bombers roared overhead and flak flew around us. My RAF friend asked if I was afraid. I answered truthfully, not more than I usually was in my day to day routine. I told him how I had found inner peace and was trying to follow what I thought God was telling me.

As we lay there we went on to talk about life's daily troubles – sex frustrations, loneliness, the lack of positive purpose in wartime. Then we were quiet, and when the all clear suddenly sounded, we were both surprised. We'd forgotten about the raid that was in progress. When we got up and looked around us we saw pieces of hot shrapnel lying all around us on the barge.

I was lucky to have several friends from the Oxford Group in Malta. The most outstanding of them was Jock Joughin, Chief Constructor at the Naval Dockyard. He was well over sixty and very deaf, but a man of great courage. When *HMS Illustrious* arrived in Malta, badly damaged and in the dockyard for repairs, the Germans made day and night attacks on her. These disrupted the repairs which were being made on her bottom, since the divers who were working under the surface, and the crew who supplied their air, paid out rope to them and tended their supplies, were all forced to leave and take shelter in the caves dug into the cliffs above the dockyard.

Jock Joughin was well aware how urgently *Illustrious* was needed back on station with the convoys carrying crucial food supplies to Malta. He decided to act. When the next alert sounded he stood on the quay and as the men ran towards the air raid shelter he called to them, asking their help to put on a diving suit. One of the divers yelled, "You are too old for that kind of work, sir. When did you last dive?"

"Oh, probably thirty years ago, but someone must go down and get this ship ready to sail. And these raids will go on every hour, killing a lot of people, until we get the ship out."

The divers and their crew looked at each other, and finally a diver said, "All right, I'll go down if you'll stay here on the pontoon. I'll feel safe with you there; no bombs ever seem to land near you."

It was true. Jock used to walk around unharmed through the air raids, partly to encourage his men, and partly because he was so deaf he didn't always hear the warning sirens.

One day Jock came aboard our ship and after looking around asked if we needed any repairs or improvements; he said he had several hundred men around in the yards with little to do. Joking, I told him that my bunk was only six feet long, and I was six feet four. His response was that he would have a crew of his men to lengthen the bed next day. What else needed doing? I listed a number of things, but said that Captain Macfarlane must authorise any such work. Jock insisted on seeing him at once.

The captain smiled when Jock made his offer, saying he couldn't authorise the company's spending the money. Jock gave a big grin; "My men need the work. Don't worry about payment – there'll be a thousand years of peace to decide who's going to pay." And a lot of useful work was done.

Another great man was Stanley Barnes, who had come to Malta before the war broke out to organise the delivery each day of pasteurised milk, in place of the raw goat's milk supplied by herds on the streets and which carried terrible disease. When war came Stanley joined the RAF and was given the responsibility in Malta of servicing the precious high octane spirit needed by the RAF and Fleet Air Arm on the island. The fuel was carried on general cargo ships in Jerry cans, because that way it had a better chance of arriving than in a tanker amidst the bombing. On the island the fuel, along with other supplies, was stored in a tunnel under a hill in the middle of the island, originally constructed for a railway line that was never completed. Stanley's courageous wife, Joyce, remained in Malta with him all through the war. She was a nursing sister at George's Hospital, overlooking Grand Harbour, the most bombed area in the island.

I also had a marvellous aunt, my father's sister, living in Malta. She ran a school for girls, the Chiswick House School, in Sliema, to which Navy, Army and Air Force families sent their daughters. Always cheerful, always working for others, she was a tower of strength to visit. And there was Commander George Laing, in charge of gunnery repair in the dockyard. His influence was felt far beyond the yard; he broadcast news talks over the *Rediffusion* Lines into every home in Malta. These talks, in which he was joined by Jock and others, did much to maintain the morale of that island at a time more dangerous and threatening than any we went through in Britain.

I learned to love the island and its people. Until then I had shared the typical superior British attitude that Eastern Mediterranean people were untrustworthy. But in wartime I saw the Maltese people teaching us what calmness, bravery and responsibility really meant. They were a joyous lot, singing, making music, laughing and appreciating their beautiful island. And this was not even their

war. They were being attacked by their nearest
relatives, the Italians. Had the Germans been
humble enough to trust the Italians with the taking
of Malta, it might have been lost to Britain. If so,
the North African campaign might have resulted
in the enemy's victory in the Middle East, cutting
off our oil supplies. As it was, the Maltese dog-
gedly resisted the Germans. German arrogance,
coupled with Maltese guts, did much to secure
Allied victory.

From Malta at last *Melbourne Star* received
orders to sail alone, running the gauntlet of
German and Italian arms, which controlled both
north and south shores of the Mediterranean. This
meant steering some fifty miles south of Sicily,
where Kesselring's "air circus", considered at that
time the most lethal air weapon in the world, was
stationed.

We sailed north of Pantellaria, a small island
with an enemy air base and a nest of motor torpedo boats, then along the enemy occupied North
African coasts of Tunisia and Algeria, to reach our
goal, Gibraltar. We were carrying a large number
of passengers, mostly servicemen and their wives
who had been a long time in Malta and were in
need of repatriation.

Wily precautions had to be taken before we left
Malta. On each side of *Melbourne Star* we fitted
large rolls of canvas, about forty feet long and
fifteen feet deep. On them was painted the name
of a French ship, with Marseilles as the port of
registry, and we flew the Vichy French flag of Ger-
man-controlled France. After passing the range of
any binoculars we unrolled the canvas, hoping that

now we would appear an innocent ally to any patrolling enemy aircraft or ships.

We had been ordered to sail along the North African coast inside the minefields, a route that had been reconnoitred by British submarines based in Malta. We had made good friends with these submarines, who enjoyed coming aboard for samples from some of the thousand cases of Bass we carried on board. As a result the submariners gave us every bit of information they had gathered of enemy minefields, ship movements and shore base gun emplacements.

We sailed in the evening and ran the gauntlet south of Sicily in the dark with no lights. Dawn heralded another beautiful day. No shipping was in sight; we might have been on a pleasure cruise. Our course took us to Bizerta, occupied by the Germans, and there we had to steam almost into the harbour to avoid the minefield.

I took over the watch at four a.m. and checked all the instruments. I was horrified to see on the echo sounder that there was only four feet of water under our bottom. I rushed into the chartroom, where the captain was resting, and said, "Sir, there's only four feet of water under the ship!" He opened his eyes wearily and replied, "Ah, that's good. We've only had eighteen inches for the last ten hours." We were that close to the coast.

We steamed into Bizerta just before dawn and as we steamed out again a signal lamp began flashing from the shore, obviously from a German post. Once again I rushed to consult Captain Macfarlane. "Sir, they're calling us from the shore. What do I do?"

Again he opened his eyes and said calmly, "Nelson had a blind eye; we might as well follow his lead." And again closed his eyes.

All was quiet until soon after dawn, when we saw a Dornier three engined flying boat taking off from near Bizerta. We kept going at fifteen knots, instead of our normal twenty, which would have revealed that we were not a slow Vichy French ship. Our guns were covered and we had painted the ship to look as old as possible. The Dornier flew around us in a great circle, probably trying to contact someone by radio to verify if the ship with our name could be in the area.

"Shall I turn out the gun crews?" I asked the captain.

"Certainly not. That would let them know we were the enemy in disguise."

Then the Dornier descended, altered course and began approaching us directly. The captain phoned the engine room, "Be ready for emergency manoeuvres." As the plane came closer we saw its bomb bay doors open and the captain told the helmsman to be ready to come hard to port. To me he said, "Let me know if you see a bomb dropping."

The Dornier was approaching us on a line from bow to stern, to make us a maximum target. I shouted, "Bomb coming." The captain quietly ordered, "Hard to starboard" and rang full astern starboard engine. The bomb fell beyond us and sank without exploding. The captain resumed course. The Dornier circled to make another run at us. The captain put on a beret and asked me, "Do I look a French captain?" Then he went out on to the wing of the bridge and shook his fist at the plane, grinning. "That should scare them away."

Apparently it did, because the Dornier made a couple more circles and then headed back to Bizerta. As soon as we could see it no longer, the captain ordered full twenty knots and said, "I think I'll have some breakfast and then some sleep."

We headed full speed for Cape de Gata on the southern tip of Spain and into the Spanish three mile limit. Almost at once a Spanish fighter plane began flying around us; Spain was neutral and kept a strict eye on all new arrivals. We welcomed its escort into Gibraltar. We spent a disturbed night in its harbour, with depth charges exploding at frequent intervals. The Germans kept a non military tanker docked across the Straits in Algeciras from which they sent frogmen at night to swim over and fix limpet mines on the bottoms of our ships. The British sent our patrol boats round the harbour dropping depth charges to discourage the frogmen.

We were glad to sail for Buenos Aires, where we were to load a cargo of meat for England. It proved to be a quiet, uneventful trip, with no passengers aboard and an opportunity to rest and relax. We needed it. On arrival in Buenos Aires we headed to the South Dock, alongside the Frigerifico Anglo, the huge abattoir freezer owned by our shipping company.

Each morning herds of cattle were delivered by rail to the paddock behind the Frigerifico; there they were coralled into narrow lanes, one beast at

a time. A man stood behind a fence above the
animals' line of sight and as each beast passed,
tapped it on the top of its head with a light hammer
and it dropped dead. Another man inserted a hook
into it as it dropped and it was carried up on a
moving belt to the abattoir.

A few hours later, the carcasses had been dis-
jointed, the meat frozen and brought down on
hooks on a runway into the ship's frozen cham-
bers. The offal was loaded separately, all neatly
packed, and the hides and fatty acid followed
shortly. By evening the entire herd was stowed
away, spotlessly and painlessly. In peacetime we
had carried meat hung on hooks and chains in the
holds, only chilled, so that it arrived in the UK in
prime condition, but in wartime we needed all the
space we could use, so the meat was deep frozen
and tightly packed. We loaded some twelve thousand tons, urgently needed by war-isolated Britain.

Our stay in Buenos Aires was not all work. On
the first night some of us younger officers went
ashore. To reach the city we had to cross a hanging
cradle bridge over the river mouth. On our return,
we decided to climb to a narrow path over the top
of the bridge. It was dangerous and not open to
the public. On the other side we were stopped by
a policeman, who asked us sternly why we had
done this. Just for fun, we told him. He gave us a
big smile; "Enjoy yourselves in BA," he said.

On our first day the naval attaché at the British
Embassy addressed all the crew members, warning
us of the danger from enemy informers. He told
us which bars and restaurants were safe and which
were not. Don't be fooled, he said, by the friendli-

ness of people; some earned money by passing information to the German Embassy. He mentioned the Boston, a café and dance hall in Boca, the suburb closest to where we were docked, as a dangerous place.

Next night, Kahn, a young Royal Artillery bombardier in charge of the ratings who manned our guns, took two of the men ashore. They saw the Boston, brightly lit and noisy with music and people. Ignoring the attaché's advice, he led the party in, saying it would be fun to pick out the spies. They sat at a table near the dance floor and ordered drinks. Soon they were joined by a pretty girl, who said to Kahn, "Move your chair back a bit, dear," and as he politely did so, she swept up her short skirt and sat on his lap. She clearly had nothing on under her skirt. Kahn was dumbfounded when she threw her arms around him, kissed him gently on the lips and said, "You are a lovely man, would you like to sleep with me?"

"No thanks," Kahn spluttered, "please go away."

The girl replied, "Oh, so you don't want me. All right, I'll go," and walked out of the restaurant. Kahn and his friends relaxed, drink up their beers and called for the bill. He reached into his pocket for his wallet. It was gone, along with his money, Army pay book, ship's pass and other papers. No doubt by next morning the German Embassy had the details of our ship on the wire to Berlin.

As in Malta, I had good friends I had met through the Oxford Group, now better known as Moral Re-Armament. Cecil Bonner, manager of the Central Argentine Railway, invited me to a

memorable luncheon at the restaurant in his headquarters. The head waiter suggested that since I
was from England I might appreciate a good beef
steak. I gladly ordered one, but when it arrived I
was startled to see it was enormous, nine inches
long, four wide and an inch thick. It was beautifully tender, cooked to a dream, but after eating
only half, I could manage no more. The hovering
head waiter was concerned – was something
wrong with the steak? I explained that my stomach
was not used to such fare. Dejected, he had it
removed and said anxiously, "I recommend our
special Strawberries Dorchester House." This, I
discovered, consisted of fresh strawberries, clotted
cream, lightly frozen and flavoured with straw-
berry liqueur. I could only manage a spoonful or
two – I fear the British lost prestige in the eyes of
the restaurant staff that day.

Cecil was a most thoughtful host, arranging a
trip on his railway to some of the beautiful
countryside, playing cricket on their ground and
giving me an understanding of Argentina's history
and people. But most of all I remember one of
our conversations about marriage. He had recently
celebrated his fortieth wedding anniversary. Theirs
had been a very happy marriage, he said. He and
his wife had had their ups and down, but no
serious troubles. Then he said, "But as I was thinking of those forty years, I realised that there was
one thing about my wife that had always niggled
me. She was so illogical.

"To run this railway I have to be logical and
systematic, but when I come home everything my
wife does is run on habit and instinct. For years

I'd tried to change her on this. On our fortieth anniversary I decided to give up trying to make her logical. Now, five months later, I've stopped trying. I realise that what I most appreciate about her is her illogicality. It's just the medicine I need to unwind me from business!"

That set me thinking about my own marriage. I knew that, like my friend, I was usually more concerned about my affairs than what was going on in Nancy's mind. She and I had met when we were both sixteen, when she visited my mother's hotel where I was working. We danced, flirted, had a good time; then she went back to Bristol, where she lived.

When I lay in hospital, with my back broken, she wrote me – the only girl who did. A couple of years later, I heard that she and her sister and two boy friends were coming to Swanage for a dance and I crashed the party and somehow persuaded the others to leave Nancy, and the two of us drove back to Bournemouth in the early hours of the morning in the mini-van I was using in my job.

It was a turning point for both of us. We'd known each other for two years, but hadn't even kissed. We sat close, I in the driver's seat, she on an empty apple crate. She became the most important person in my life. Another two summers went by, and Nancy came again to stay at Linden Hall with her parents and visited me in Swanage, where I was working.

By that time I had learned the importance of being quiet and listening to God's guidance. I was clear that we should marry, although we would have very little income on which to live, and my relatives were opposed to the idea. I talked with Nancy on the phone and she agreed to come to Bournemouth to be married.

The event was far from romantic. I was working for a greengrocer at the time and asked my friend Fergie to escort Nancy to the Registry Office – we couldn't afford a big church wedding. I arrived late, still in my working clothes. The registrar told us we needed a second witness, so I went out and invited a passing ice cream delivery boy to be a witness.

Then I had to hurry back to work to take care of the evening deliveries, and Fergie took Nancy for a wedding breakfast in Bobby's Restaurant – for which she paid, until next day, when I collected my pay. She also had to pay for her Woolworth wedding ring.

The first few years of our marriage rested on equally shaky foundations. Nancy and I lived briefly in a friend's home until mother located a large house owned by an elderly widow who was willing to rent it to us for a modest sum. We had no furniture, but mother and friends lent us enough to furnish two rooms.

Then Uncle Leo, mother's brother, went to an auction and bid fifty pounds for everything. There were no other bidders and he had it all shipped over to our house, saying he would pay us a modest amount as a "storage fee". We then set about finding lodgers who would rent our unused rooms, now furnished with uncle's old fashioned furniture. We landed up with some odd lodgers – a German taxi driver with an English wife, a woman cook from a nearby café, and an actor who never seemed to be able to come up with his monthly rent.

By this time Nancy's long pregnancy was making it impossible for her to take care of the big house and she took on a young Turkish girl to help with the housework. The baby was overdue and at the doctor's suggestion I started driving her over bumpy roads to hasten the event. As I worked long hours I became increasingly worried about Nancy until, one morning, my boss came over to me and said in sepulchural tones, "When you've finished with this customer I have something very serious to tell you." When I hurried over to him, convinced that the worst must have happened to Nancy, he seized both my hands, started dancing and told me I was a father of a baby girl.

A few months later, the managing director of a group of several hotels where I had worked drove up to the store in his big white Humber Snipe, told me to get in and offered me a job. He had been strongly opposed to my marrying and had in fact eased me out of my hotel job, saying a young man could not learn the hotel trade and look after a wife and family at the same time. He had just brought a hotel in Swanage and needed someone to supervise the major renovation of the hotel.

I gladly accepted, spent the next months there, with Nancy and the baby living in comfortable quarters and with good food. When the work ended I moved back to mother's hotel to work during the summer season, and it was during that time that a senior hotel man suggested I spend some months in Germany for further training in hotel management. I left Nancy and our daughter for the best part of a year, and after that joined the merchant service and had seen little of them since.

I had missed Nancy all through my long weeks at sea, during the tense stay in Malta, and here in Buenos Aires, despite the pleasant activities. On early morning watches I would find myself thinking, what time is it where Nancy is, what is she doing, is she happy, is she as lonely as I am, is she still faithful to me? I could easily drive myself into a frenzy. Then I would stop. Something inside myself seemed to say, "Forget yourself; everyone on this ship feels the same way as you. Think about the people around you."

I was coming to accept that the quiet voice inside was more than just me; it was God speaking, directing me out of my selfish concerns and making me aware of the needs of others.

While in Buenos Aires I had a startling experience of being propelled into the lives of others. Among those I met was the wife of a banker who invited me to her home to meet people who had become interested in Moral Re-Armament. At an informal meeting that evening she asked me to speak to them about myself, something I did not feel like doing, especially in that company, which was of a social level well above the one in which I moved. As others were speaking, and I was trying to jot down in a notebook what I might say, I became very conscious of the lady sitting next to me. Why, I wondered, did she have such dark rings around her eyes? I even wrote that question down in my notebook.

When the meeting ended, everyone except this

lady and I, got up to get coffee. She and I sat, and nervously I handed her my notebook and pointed to my query. She read it and started to cry. Then she pulled herself together and said, "I'm in desperate trouble. I need help badly and can't talk to anyone here. Would you come to my apartment and see if you can help me?"

I was nervous about being involved, but she seemed so distressed I decided to go with her. At her home she started to tell her story. Ann was the daughter of British expatriates who had returned to Britain. Her husband, an Argentinian of German descent had died, leaving her two sons. She had done her best to raise the boys, but it was an unhappy time. Then she had become very friendly with the rector of the Anglican church of which she was a member; he was single, in his late forties, and out of the blue had asked her to marry him. After much thought she had agreed, at least partly because she felt the boys needed a father.

Ann soon became worried because her husband never touched her and after a couple of years moved out of their bedroom and joined her fourteen year old son. She thought this very odd, but life continued happily until, a few months later, she overheard two women church members gossiping; one said in a low voice to her friend, "The Rector is such a nice man, it's a pity he is a homosexual." She could not bring herself to believe the woman, but nor could she reject her suspicions. For the past few months life had been miserable.

I asked her why she had not talked with her husband and she replied that she had really nothing to go on, and he would be so hurt.

Very soon the Rector came home and, seeing me, said to his wife, "Ah, I see you have a guest. Excuse me, I'm very tired, I'm off to bed."

I jumped up and said, "Please, Rector, don't go. Your wife has been telling me things she should have been telling you long ago, and I think she should tell you now, before you go to bed."

Ann protested, and her husband made it clear he did not want to hear anything from her. But I kept insisting and finally she came out with the whole story. Then there was a silence.

"Your turn, Rector," I said. "Your wife has suffered agony for long enough. You must tell her the truth."

He looked up at me and said, "It's something I've wanted to do for some years, but never had the courage. Yes, I am a homosexual, but I've never touched either of the boys. But I've been deeply disturbed by my relationship with Ann for a long time."

I said to Ann, "I think it's time for you to go to bed," and she went.

I said to the Rector, "If you haven't had a homosexual relationship with the boys, who have you had one with?"

He told me about his relations with some of the men in the church; said he was ashamed about it, but had no cure. I told him my belief that if he would take time to listen to God, God would surely tell him what to do. He said he was ready for anything to have the mess cleared up.

We sat quietly with pen and paper. He wrote nothing, and I was saying to myself, "Am I making a fool of myself and of the Rector?" Then he started to write and wrote for a long time.

"I believe God has spoken to me," he said at last, and went on to say that the marriage must be annulled; it had never been consummated; he must resign his position and leave the country, must make an appointment with his bishop and make his confession.

I left and never saw him again. Some years later, I ran across Ann in London and she told me that the Rector had done everything he had told me he would. He had become a new man, taking a curacy thousands of miles away in a church where he had become a great inspiration. She had eventually met a fine man and married him.

Our journey home was a joy, sailing on our own, calling at Jamaica for bunker fuel, then on to Liverpool. Everything was fine until we ran into trouble as we approached Rathlin Island, off the north Irish cost, and headed into the narrows between the south of Scotland and the north of Ireland. It was the area where outward bound convoys assumed their stations before sailing out into the Atlantic.

I was on watch, intently alert because ships carried no lights. Suddenly the forecastle look-out called on the phone, "Small craft close in on the starboard bow, apparently crossing our bow." At that moment we saw the eerie outline of a small ship, much too close to avoid by any alteration of course or reduction of speed. I could now make out her outline, a Flower class corvette. It disappeared under our bow and we waited for the crunch as I thought in horror of the sinking of a much needed escort ship and, even worse, the drowning of a hundred fellow seamen. It appeared again on our port bow and rushed past, not more than fifty feet from the side of our bridge.

We docked in Liverpool and I went on leave to visit my brother Pat, who was staying with friends in London. I was not feeling well, and Pat insisted I see a friend, a renowned Harley Street surgeon, Campbell Milligan. The next thing I knew was that I was in an ambulance headed for hospital with a bad case of double pneumonia.

Torpedoings, bombings and the rest, it seemed, had taken their toll on my body. It was a Catholic hospital and I woke up one morning with a little St Christopher medallion in my hand. One of the Irish nurses had put it there – they thought I was going to die. When Dr Milligan arrived and I showed it to him, he grinned. "I only just stopped them from ordering a box for you! I have more faith than they do!" Despite that, the nurses were charming, devoted and took wonderful care of me.

Nancy's parents invited me to stay at their home in Bristol to convalesce and for the first time I began to get to know them. They were very respectable and highly respected, which I was not, but we got on very well. While there I took the opportunity to attend lectures at a hospital on first aid and health care; there are few doctors available on freighters, and in order to be qualified as a ship's master I needed to be able to take care of health emergencies in a crew.

As soon as I regained my strength I went to Liverpool to join the *Tudor Star*. I found her undergoing an annual inspection and painting of her bottom, rudder and propellor. She lay in a double dry dock, which she shared with a destroyer. The next night the "Jerries" dropped a delayed action bomb which landed unexploded, wedged into the bottom of the dock, partially underneath the destroyer, damaging some of her plates.

Over the side of our ship at a safe distance, we nervously watched a bomb disposal gang arrive, a young subaltern and three scruffy looking seamen, who then sat around the bomb brewing tea while the subaltern sat on the bomb and listened to it with something like a stethoscope. Two of them went back to their van and returned with a pneumatic drill, with which they started to dig the bomb out of the bottom of the dock. When they had it dug loose, a mobile crane picked it up and set it on an open van, which drove it through Liverpool to Crosby Sands, where it was exploded. The steadiness of those men in the face of danger made me feel very humble.

Day after day, as we lay in the drydock, we lived in primitive conditions, with no light, heat or water. Food was cooked for us over a charcoal fire in the galley; our only lavatory was a public one on the dock. To take a bath I had to fill buckets of boiling water from a drum on a brazier on the after-deck, carry them amidships and pour them into a bath. For cold water I had to go on to the quay and fill a bucket from a fire hydrant.

One night, when I was on duty, with only one cadet sleeping aboard, and oil lights, I decided to take a bath. I had filled two buckets with scalding water and was carrying them across the deck when

I tripped on a hose and fell heavily on one knee, hitting it against a protruding deck plate edge.

I struggled to my cabin, with the knee swelling fast, and called for the cadet to get me a taxi and told him to inform the duty officer of *California Star*, which lay nearby, and ask him to keep an eye on my ship while I was at the hospital. Before the taxi arrived, the captain of the *California* came to see me. He was a jovial character known throughout the fleet as "Bullshit". He examined my knee and said, "No need to worry. It's not serious. There's no need to go to hospital."

He was not my captain, so I told him without hesitation that I was going for an X-ray. His reply was that if I did so he would report me to the Superintendent's Department. I told him angrily that it was my leg and I left as soon as the taxi came.

At the hospital I was delighted to find that the doctor on duty was Jack Gibson, whom I'd met before. He took some X-rays, announced that I had fractured my knee cap, and set it in plaster. I returned to the *California* and told the duty officer the news and he agreed to look after the *Tudor* for me. I collected some belongings and drove to a small rooming house belonging to a friend.

When I phoned the Superintendent's Department next morning, they told me they'd heard about my accident from the captain of the *California*. Next day the marine superintendent phoned back to ask if I would be rejoining the *Tudor* that day. He must know otherwise he would have to find a replacement.

"I can't,' I replied. "I have a broken knee cap and my leg's in plaster."

"The captain of the *California* had told us about that. It was a good idea for you to take the weekend off, but now we need you back."

I was staggered and repeated for him the extent of my injuries. He came back with, "We know your doctor is a friend and he's fixed things for you."

I was enraged and yelled at him that he'd got everything wrong. He replied in a cold voice that I would be hearing from them.

Next day I received a letter from the Personnel Office saying that my services were no longer required and that I was transferred to the "pool", the Merchant Navy establishment which found officers and crew for ships. I went to the "pool" in London and they sent me to their doctor, who wrote me off totally unfit for sea service for at least three months. There would be no pay for me, so I phoned the Blue Star Line, who told me I was transferred to Workmen's Compensation, because I was not on the payroll of an active ship at the time of the accident – the *Tudor Star* was only a "warehouse" while in dry dock and I was classified as a warehouseman entitled to only thirty-five shillings per week. I now had to find food and lodging and everything on about one tenth of my regular pay.

I decided to seek help from our Officers' Association. The general secretary, Douglas Tennant, was an ex-ship officer of great ability and character. He had stood up for the rights of seamen while at sea and continued to do so when too old to

sail. He was furious at what I told him, but also
frustrated because Blue Star had been within the
letter of the law. The only way was to change the
law, and that cost money. He could not use the
Association's funds for the benefit of one member;
it might run into thousands of pounds.

I jumped in and said I understood that, but go
ahead and fight it. If it took ten thousand pounds,
never mind, I'd pay for it, if it took the rest of my
life.

Doug looked at me for a long time and said,
"You would, too, wouldn't you? Leave it to me."

I went home without much hope and waited for
work on another ship, but there was a large "pool"
of unemployed officers because so many ships had
been sunk. One day Doug phoned me to say he'd
won the case.

"You'll be getting a cheque from the Blue Star
Line for back pay and living expenses."

"How on earth did you achieve that?" I asked.

"Well, when all else failed, I went to A. P. Herbert, MP and got him to raise the question in the
House of Commons, and the law was changed."
A. P. Herbert was a household name at the time
– writer, humorist and playwright as well as MP.

Sure enough, a few days later, a handsome
cheque arrived from Blue Star. Next morning,
Captain Angus, the Line's marine superintendent,
telephoned: "I want to thank you very much for
what you have done. You've made my job a lot
easier." I asked what I had done.

"First, no one in my office gave the order for
you to be transferred to the 'pool'. It was done by a
junior clerk in personnel who followed the routine

legal position. I'm very sorry it happened to you. Further, this law was wrong and we in this department had raised the point with the authorities for many years, but had not been able to achieve anything. You have got the law altered and that will be a great help to us and to all seamen."

"But the Union and Doug Tennant did all the work," I protested.

"I know, but it was your willingness and determination to fight that made it possible – so I am told."

Then he asked me which ship I would like to join. I couldn't believe my ears, but he said he meant it, and added, "Any time you need a job, just apply to us."

There was an interesting sequel years later. In 1955 I was in limbo between jobs and wrote to Blue Star Line to ask if they had any jobs of interest for me. They wrote back saying that I was on pay for the next day and I should go to see one of their superintendents to find out what he could do for me.

5

Long wait for a new ship

I was next ordered to join the Canadian Pacific's *Benverhill*, sailing for Halifax, Nova Scotia. A number of us who had been torpedoed or for some other reason had no ship were being sent to Canada to await the building of ships there or in the United States. The *Benverhill* was a transatlantic cargo liner originally designed to carry twelve passengers; some of her cargo space had been converted to dormitories to serve eighty passengers. Mine had no portholes, only one door, and should we be torpedoed, only ladders to climb to escape.

Soon after we sailed most of us headed for bed. I was exhausted from several changes of trains, lugging too much baggage since I did not know whether I would find myself in tropical climes or Icelandic waters, nor how long I would be away. I was accustomed to praying before sleeping, but this evening I sat on my top bunk, scared to get down on my knees and look a fool. Next night, I said to myself, "What the hell!" and knelt and said my childlike prayers. I don't believe anyone even noticed.

After a rough voyage of more than a week we docked at Halifax and were taken on a special train to Montreal and boarded in the Dorchester Hotel, which was filled with ships' officers awaiting ships. We had expected to stay a couple of nights, then dash off to join a ship, but were told we would have to wait around for several weeks – in fact the ship to which I was allocated had not even had her keel laid yet. I shared a common bathroom and adjoining rooms with Bill, a third mate. Bill was a lad with initiative; within a few days he found himself a job in the glove department of Simpson's, a prestigious department store. Within a week he was promoted to manager of the glove department, until he sailed four months later. As soon as he returned to Montreal for his next ship he resumed the job for several more months.

I soon became bored with sitting around Montreal and followed his example. I walked into Scott's, at that time the leading restaurant, and was interviewed by Mr Waters, the manager. He could not believe that the young man wearing a second mate's uniform could be a trained cook. He smiled politely and said, "We are fully staffed, and in any case you have no proof of your ability, nor any references."

As I walked into the Dorchester, tired after a fruitless round of interviews, a loud-speaker was calling my name. I was wanted on the phone. Mr Waters asked, "What do you know about hot sandwich counter work?"

I could only guess what such a counter was, but answered, "I haven't had a lot of experience, but I'm sure I could cope." He said the hot counter sandwich cook had not arrived; could I come right over?

"I'll come. But I need a bath and to freshen up. What about a meal?"

"You'll get a meal here. Please come as soon as you can."

When I arrived twenty minutes later I was fitted up with a white apron and high hat and stood behind the counter. A man walked in, sat down and called, "Gimme a Western sandwich."

I wondered what the hell a Western sandwich was and turned to the dish washing woman and quietly asked her.

"Ich kann nicht English sprechen," she said.

Luckily I spoke German and understood her description. I made the sandwich with a flourish, gave it to the man, accepted his cash and he wolfed it down and was walking out when he ran into Mr Waters and greeted him; "Thank God you've got a cook at last who can make a proper Western sandwich."

Gretel, my dish wash lady, and I had a good laugh over that. I learned that she was a refugee from Hitler. I worked at the counter five nights and was then promoted head of the evening shift in the main kitchen. Before long, a chief engineer and third mate joined me on my shift at Scott's. When we all had to leave suddenly to join ships, the manager threatened to post a notice, "Ships sailed, restaurant closed."

In Montreal, as in other cities I was visiting, I

found Moral Re-Armament friends. Among them was the Webster family. Andrew, a builder's merchant, told me about a campaign the government was conducting to save fuel, precious in the city's freezing winter. They were urging him and other builders to insulate the cavity walls of houses with Micafill, a light mineral product of which there was an ample supply available. Andrew told me he had a long waiting list of homeowners eager for the insulation, but he lacked the labour. That evening I talked with a chief-engineer waiting ship; he visited Mr Webster and soon there was a gang of waiting seamen gainfully employed on the urgently needed project.

Another delightful family was the Hallwards, who made their beautiful home near Mount Royal available to me. Bernard was chairman of a family paper manufacturing company and his wife Alice was the daughter of the proprietor of the leading newspaper. One day I walked into the home with an illustrated Soviet magazine. Bernard picked it up and stared at the cover. "See that textile mill? I know that place. In fact, I was engineer in charge of building it about 1913."

I politely suggested he was mistaken; the magazine says it was completed last year. "Is that so?" said my host. "Well, I assure you it was built by British workers in 1913. I recall that we installed three hundred weaving machines. I think I still have the plans and photos of the plant in the attic."

Sure enough, there they were, except that the factory was painted a different colour and the workers' clothes were an older style. Bernard got a lot of amusement from the fact that after nearly thirty years his factory was now being touted as an advertisement for today's Communism.

From the Hallwards, Websters and others I heard about a summer-long Moral Re-Armament gathering being held on Mackinac Island, which stood at the junction of two of the Great Lakes, Huron and Michigan, close to the US-Canadian border. I was eager to take part in it, and as soon as I'd saved enough money I made arrangements to go. Officially we officers who were waiting for ships were not supposed to leave Canada, but the regulation was not enforced, and I obtained a permit from the immigration office for a limited stay in the US and set out for Mackinac.

This was not the first time I had participated in an Oxford Group Moral Re-Armament activity. Back in 1935, soon after my first encounter, I took a very minor part in a campaign they were conducting in Belfast, and later that year I was invited to join an international team who were holding meetings in Switzerland. Frank Buchman, the initiator of the Oxford Group, had been invited by President Benes of Czechoslovakia and Carl Hambro, President of the Norwegian Parliament – both prominent men in the League of Nations – to meet League members. It was a very difficult time for the League as the Italian delegation had just walked out when the League expressed concern at Mussolini's threat to invade Ethiopia. My contribution was modest; I carried bags, parked cars, ran errands. But I also observed at first hand the impact of this force of some fifty men and women on the living and thinking of all kinds of people, for ordinary citizens to international statesmen. The Oxford Group team brought a new dimension of hope, personal responsibility and moral challenge into a climate of despondency.

From Geneva we went to Berne and then on to Zurich. Thousands of people flocked into public meetings. I found myself called on to speak in a cathedral, a small church and in a stock exchange, all within the same day. I spoke very briefly, along with some twenty others, and my message was that after I had put my will into God's hands, to try to do what he wanted, rather than going my own selfish way, relations with my family and my fellow workers were radically improved.

While in Zurich I had a memorable talk with Frank Buchman. A message reached me late one evening that he wished to see me before he left for the US next morning. I found him sitting up in bed in his hotel room, with aides hurrying around packing his papers and belongings. He asked me to sit by his bed and told me he wanted to ask me four questions; "I don't want any answers right now. First, are you happy working with us here? Second, are you cheating? Do you think God wants you to be here working with us? And finally, Have you any money?"

I started to answer, but he said, "Please just think about it. Ask God to tell you what he wants. Now, I must say goodbye, and blessings to you."

As I walked back to my hotel I felt angry about being hauled out in the middle of the night to be asked those odd questions. I reached into my pocket for a packet of cigarettes and suddenly realised I'd been cheating. I had seen how frugally my teammates were living, with few financial resources; none of them smoked and I wanted to give up cigarettes, but still smoked secretly. I was cheating.

I asked myself, was I happy with this crowd? Yes and no. I was not fully committed, as they were, more of a fascinated spectator. Did I think God wanted me to be totally committed? Oddly enough, I did; not necessarily to travel around together, as they were doing, but to live a life committed permanently, not to a church or a movement, but to doing His will.

Later that day I threw my packet of cigarettes into the lake and from then on lost my craving for them. I had a few pounds from my mother tucked away in my wallet against any financial emergency. I decided to pitch in this money to help with the expenses of our group. Since then I have never felt constrained by money from doing what I felt was right.

I arrived on Mackinac Island to find an extended conference in full swing. The five hundred or so men and women had come from all parts of the US and Canada, as well as from some other countries. Some parents had brought their children, and the whole gathering had more of the atmosphere of a family than a conference. Everyone pitched in to take care of the housekeeping chores – cooking, dish washing, and so on. I found myself on a dish wash crew with a great variety of men – business and professional men, college kids, auto workers. I learned as much about them, their homes and communities as I did from the talks given at the meetings.

Again, it was conversation with Frank Buchman

that stands out most in my mind. He invited me to join him in a couple of deck chairs on a lawn looking across the lake. He asked me news of several mutual friends whom I'd been seeing in England, then handed me a copy of the *New York Herald Tribune* and picked up the *New York Times*. "While we talk," he said, "we can read." We read and talked; he turned to me at one point and said, "Tell me where we're going wrong here." I was startled and said nothing.

Frank went on, "Coming here fresh, you must notice things that are wrong quicker than you see what is being achieved." I said anything I criticised seemed trivial, but he encouraged me to speak out.

"I noticed newspapers lying all over the place when I first walked into the lobby."

Frank laughed and said, "Trust the English, with their neat little island. But you're right; we must do something about it. What else?"

"I'm the only person in uniform here." He encouraged me to think of ways of getting others. What else?

I said tentatively, "Everyone seems to get on well here, but men and women seem very stiff with one another."

"That's something that's concerned me for some time. Having never been married, I'm not good at solving that."

I was struck by Buchman's eagerness to receive suggestions and criticisms. I remember, too, his final words before we were summoned to lunch. "You have to remember that the United States is not a country like Britain. It's a continent, a federation of states. We think differently about many things and see everything in a bigger perspective. We need to learn again from the ideas that the British brought here when they first came; and you British need a wider perspective."

I was interested that Buchman followed through on some of the points I had raised. A group of women consulted me about ideas for a skit they mounted for the conference dealing in a humorous way with mess in the buildings; a young journalist picked my brains about a memo to be sent out to servicemen at various bases inviting them to Mackinac.

My immigration permit was about to expire, so I said my farewells and was given a big send-off on the ferry to the mainland. There, in St Ignace, I hitch-hiked a ride to the Canadian border at Sault Ste Marie, picked up by a Chicago family of Greek background. I described to them what I'd seen at Mackinac and what I felt about its significance. You are living in a deeply divided country, I told them. Most of you are far removed from the struggle in Europe and do not understand the evil force that is taking over the minds and hearts of people, as well as their nations. Most of you want to stay out of war, which is understandable. Some of you want America involved, but are not really prepared to pay the price. So Americans are at each others' throats. The people I've been visiting on that island have committed themselves to the moral and spiritual rearmament of America and the world. They believe that whether the US goes to war or not, the nation must prepare itself for leadership in a different kind of world.

They asked where I was headed and when I told

them I would be waiting for my ship to be built, the father asked why I hadn't stayed on longer at Mackinac.

"My permit to stay in the US has run out."

"We'll soon fix that," he said. "Come with me to the immigration office."

I followed him. He talked with an official, gave his credentials as a sponsor for me, and I was handed an extended visa.

"Go back to the island," said the Greek. "It sounds like the most important thing happening in the USA. They need all the help they can get," and handed me some dollars to help me on my way. My return to Mackinac was hilarious. All those who had bidden me goodbye were astounded to see me walk into supper. "Did the Germans sink that ferry to the mainland?" one of them asked.

At last I received instructions to travel to Vancouver to stand by a ship being built in the Burrard Dry Docks. I had been looking forward for some years to a chance to make the journey across Canada and now enjoyed the train ride on the Canadian Pacific Railway. I was awed by the vast expanse of the prairies, a mind boggling sight to eyes accustomed to the scenery of a tight little island. The train moved slowly and with long stops at the major stations, a good opportunity to get the feel of the land. Past the prairies at last, we entered the Rockies, even more grand and rugged than the Swiss Alps, with which I was familiar.

I made friends with the black sleeping car attendant, the first time I'd had the opportunity to get to know a black man well. He was a very good bridge player and I partnered him for part of each day in a competitive foursome, which we usually won.

By the time we arrived in Vancouver I was becoming nervous, feeling in a strange part of the world, knowing nothing about the ship I was joining or where we would be headed. I was expected at the Phyllis Court, a quiet residential hotel where all the officers of my new ship were staying. I met the captain, a seventy-year-old Norwegian by birth, now a naturalised British subject. Captain Poulsen was the first man I had ever met who smoked his pipe upside down. Each day I and my fellow officers walked around the ship and "inspected" the work being done. My experience of shipbuilding was so limited I could contribute nothing, but the knowledge I gained stood me in good stead later.

The ship, newly named *Fort Halkett*, was a Fort "boat", the forerunner of the Liberty ship, sometimes described as the most valuable object in the winning of World War II, since without it the lifeline of men and material from the United States to Britain could not have existed. The Fort boats were a modernisation of the typical coast tramp built in the port cities of Britain's North-East. They were single screw, up-and-down steam engines, coal burning, of about eight thousand tons, well built unexciting ships.

By the time the ship neared completion and then went on sea trials I was getting to know the officers and crew. Like myself, they were mostly company men whose ships had been torpedoed. Most of them were from a Canadian Pacific ship, the *Winnipeg*. The captain and chief engineer were from

Denholm's, the company designated by the Ministry of Transport to run the ship.

The time finally arrived when I boarded the *Fort Halkett* and struggled up the long gangway ladder, barely able to haul my three large bags. Looking up, I saw Captain Poulsen looking down from the deck. "Ah, I see you're a lazy young man," he remarked. Taken aback, I asked him what he meant. "Struggling up the gangway with all those packages because you are too lazy to make two trips."

The chief mate was an austere man from the Cairn Line, very neat and efficient, the second mate was the opposite, a jovial Welshman. I was third mate. As soon as we sailed, all of us were very busy familiarising ourselves with everything on the ship.

We sailed to New Westminster, a short distance up river, and then across to Port Alberni on Vancouver Island to load lumber. We loaded sawn timber night and day, filling the holds and then piling stacks on deck until the lumber stood some thirty feet high. By the time the work was finished, to reach the fore and aft ends of the ship we had to climb on top of the timber and walk through an alleyway between rope safety lines which swayed as the ship rolled.

The stacks of timber were lashed with chains made fast to the bulwarks at the sides of the ship with great bottle screws. These screws were old fashioned devices which could be tightened very simply by inserting and turning a metal bar. Many is the time I've said a prayer of thanks to its inventor as I've gone around in a storm checking the lashings.

We had another item quietly loaded aboard before we left Burrard Dry Dock. Our ship had been chosen to try our some secret weaponry at sea. The weapons were discreetly fitted and covered, with instructions that they were not to be uncovered until we had passed through the Panama Canal. I had received a certificate after passing a Ship's Defense Course and was therefore designated the gunnery officer, although my knowledge was elementary.

We sailed down the Washington and Oregon coasts in fog so thick that crewmen walking over the timber on the way aft to their quarters were blotted from view. This was before the days of radar, and navigation relied on radio signals. At intervals down the coast radio stations transmitted identification signals which our young wireless operator picked up on his radio direction finder. The ship's safety lay in his hands and he was understandably scared since this was the first time he had used the equipment in earnest. His job was not an easy one, since the direction finder was less than precise and radio signals of all kinds filled the air, already noisy with atmospherics.

I was designated to work with him and had less experience than he had. Compounding our concern, the coast was dotted with scores of islands. This was unfamiliar territory to Captain Poulsen and all of us. Lookouts peered anxiously ahead and every two minutes our fog horn blasted away. The whole ship's company was tense. It was with great relief that we hailed the lifting of the fog off the Californian coast.

By contrast, our passage through the Panama Canal was relaxed and cheerful, with beautiful weather and safe and easy steaming. We sunbathed as we headed up through the Caribbean and past Jamaica, between Cuba and Haiti, up through the Bahamas and along the Florida coast. The captain and I spent a good deal of time putting a fresh coat of paint on the superstructure of the ship. "This ship was built too quickly," he said, "and they don't put enough paint on her. She'll be a rust bucket in no time." I learned the lesson and used it when taking on new ships. You could always tell those which had been over-painted on their first trip from those which had not.

In the Caribbean we tried out our secret weaponry. There were two types of guns. On the focsle was something called a pillar box, and that was what it looked like. The gunner sat inside, controlling the gun's elevation with one hand and its direction with the other, using eye shooting sights. He fired by pushing a foot pedal. The missiles were rockets, about six feet in length and in diameter about the size of a tin of fruit. Twelve of them were placed in open sided racks on each side of the gun, which, when fired, launched all of them in pattern formation to bring down enemy planes. That was the theory. In practice, when the rockets were fired they sent out a huge flame from their rear, taking the paint off the equipment and the skin off any loader fool enough to be standing behind it.

The second weapon was basically similar to the

first, but was designed to be fired from a distance. Larger rocket racks on this weapon were placed on the wings of the bridge, some sixty feet apart, and a control center had been fitted on the "monkey island", a raised platform on top of the wheelhouse. From here the rockets, thirty feet away, were supposed to be elevated, trained on target and fired. There were no silicon chips in those days to take the place of the mechanical controls on this complicated piece of machinery. Our gunner's mate, a retired naval gunnery rating recalled from retirement, and I gingerly unwrapped the machine and studied the secret operations manual that accompanied it. We spent many off-watch hours trying to make it work, without any success.

When we reached New York we were ordered to dock in the Brooklyn Naval Yard, an unusual berth for a merchant ship, perhaps due to our "secret weapons". On arrival I immediately called the emergency number listed in our documents and later that morning a large car pulled up with two US naval officers. They came to my cabin, looked at the documents and said this was on the Top Secret list and nothing they could handle. They'd only heard rumours about it as the Navy's latest wonder aircraft weapon. They would have to summon experts from the Chrysler Corporation in Detroit, the makers of the weapon.

After they had left, the gunner's mate came to see me. He was sure, he said, that the only reason the control didn't work was because the spring on the turning mechanism was too small. We were in the US Navy Yard and they must have springs of the right size. We made a foray into the Yard and told a foreman-type what we wanted; he directed us to the store, which had a vast number of springs, but none long enough for our requirements. Back aboard I asked one of our engineers whether he could operate a spring making machine. He said, "Sure I can, if you can find me the machine and the metal." We took him down to the store and the storekeeper and engineer disappeared into a workshop together.

Back on the ship I found two even higher ranking naval officers from the US Ordnance Department in Detroit. They came into my cabin and we closed the door for security. Out came the manual once more and the officers pored over it. The one with the most rings asked, "Commander, have you ever seen anything like this before?"

"I have not; most interesting."

As they continued to study it, I asked if they could advise me on how to make the weapon work. They could not, but the commander said he would be grateful for a report on how well it worked, when we had it operating. While I was entertaining our defense experts with drinks before they left, there was a knock on the door and the engineer came in, placed a small spring on my desk and left. I said nothing about it to the officers, since we were not supposed to have dealings with the Navy Dockyards.

The gunner's mate and I were bursting to try out the spring, but since the weapon was so secret we were not supposed to uncover it while in port. As soon as we were at sea we fired a couple of practice salvos; the spring worked perfectly. But the flash-back was so fierce that it was impossible for anyone to stay on the bridge. We covered the weapon again. For us this was more than academic research; we were sailing into an area in which ships were being sunk every day by bombs, and we had no other anti-aircraft defense.

When we eventually arrived in the UK we requested a Royal Navy Ordnance officer to examine the weapon. His response – "Oh, yes, I received a memo about these the other day. They are being abandoned as being too dangerous for shipboard use. I'll send down some men with welding equipment to cut them off and send them to the scrap yard." So much for our air defense.

While still in New York I met the British consul, Jim Marjoribanks, brother of a good friend of mine. His family had relatives and friends in the UK. They asked whether I would be willing to take some Christmas presents to them. Of course I agreed; everything in Britain was in short supply, and presents such as these would be especially welcome. Shortly afterwards, on returning to the *Fort Halkett* in the Navy Yard, I found a large notice pinned to the door of my cabin: "Lootenant Foss visits New York. His fan club has been to visit."

In my cabin were some packing cases and when I opened them I found a couple of turkeys, oranges and lemons, boxes of chocolates, nylon stockings and all kinds of goodies. They had come from Jim Marjoribanks. The second mate told me that a Navy van had arrived and said he had a number of items on the secret list for "Lootenant Foss".

He had unlocked my cabin and two US Navy

ratings had carried a number of packages aboard
and dumped them there and driven away. I hurried
to the telephone to thank Jim and asked why they
had arrived in a Navy van. He said that a commercial van had been turned away from the yard for
security reasons, so he had rung the admiral in
charge and the admiral had given orders for a
priority navy van and had added some goodies of
his own. I was a little apprehensive about the
official reaction to all these Christmas presents
when we reached the UK. Some of these items were
on the official forbidden list for imports, and the
value of imports was limited to twenty five pounds
per person.

I soon forgot about that problem as we faced
the austerities of a North Atlantic winter crossing.
From New York we sailed to Halifax, Nova Scotia
to join a convoy, then steamed out into a cold,
snowy and rough ocean. Our convoy of some
hundred ships covered about five square miles; our
speed set at that of our slowest ship, six knots.
After three days the wind dropped and so did the
temperature and we were cutting our way through
thin sea ice. Our Canadian escort handed us over
to the British, which included an ancient battleship. We knew what that meant – that the Germans probably had a battleship which had joined
the submarine wolf packs in their convoy hunting.

Then came a force ten storm, with mountainous
waves, and the naval escort ordered our convoy to
heave to, not an easy manoeuvre to execute without collisions between ships in close formation,
scarcely able to see each other amidst the flying
spray and gigantic rollers. At dawn I was on watch

and was relieved that the storm had blown itself
out, but when I looked around above the rollers I
could see only one ship, the *Cornerbrook*. During
the night the senior escort must have signalled the
order to proceed, but we had not seen the coloured
lights. I called the captain and he came on the
bridge with a sealed envelope only to be opened
in such an emergency. It contained the secret route
of the convoy. We set out at full speed to catch up
with it.

An hour later the wireless operator brought us
a signal that a ship in the convoy had been torpedoed. It was the ship that had been next to us
on our port side. We continued on course and that
evening we received another signal, "US merchant
ship *City of Flint*, number eleven in convoy, torpedoed." The message then continued in uncoded
words with the exact position of the ship. That
seemed very stupid to us.

The second mate said to me, "So now all the
German submarines, aircraft and raiders will know
where the convoy is and will home in on it. We
will come up behind and be a sitting duck, bound
to be torpedoed."

I said, "Why don't we suggest to the captain
that we go another route and avoid the convoy?"

"I think it would be better if you suggested it."

Later, on watch I did that. The captain said, "I
can't do that. I have clear instructions to follow,"
and went below. But at midnight, as I was going
off watch, he came to the bridge and asked the
second mate, who was coming on watch, what he
thought of my suggestion.

"Sir," said the second mate, "If we were to go

south for twelve hours, due east until we were twenty miles from the Irish coast, and then steam north and in through the Western Approaches, we would be there before the convoy."

The captain, looking his seventy years, stood shaking his head. "I don't know, I don't know." He went below; at two a.m. he came back on the bridge and said, "I think you and third mate are right. I've had several signals from the wireless operator of sinkings in the convoy."

We set off at full speed on the new course, picked up the Irish coast and turned north. We were met by a corvette on patrol not far from Londonderry. She signalled, asking what ship we were and where we came from. When we replied she answered that our convoy was not due for four days. We explained what had happened and the corvette replied, "You'll be in trouble. Proceed to Bangor Bay to anchor and wait orders."

We crept into Bangor Bay through thick fog, dropped anchor and everyone had a chance to sleep. Anchored near us were two minesweepers, *Gavotte* and *Minuet*. Just before dawn we were entertained by the following classic exchange on their loudhailers:

"*Gavotte, Gavotte*, this is *Minuet* calling. Can you hear me?"

"Yes, *Minuet*, I hear you."

"*Gavotte*, aren't you supposed to move off at six a.m.?'

"*Minuet*, from *Gavotte*, I did move off at six a.m."

"Why did you not light your stern light so I could see you moving off?"

"I did."

"I couldn't see it."

"Of course you didn't. It's not meant to be seen. It might give our position away to the enemy."

Eventually we received orders to proceed down the Irish Sea and around Land's End to Southampton. This was a departure from routine, which since the occupation of France had been to avoid the risky English Channel. We set off in a small convoy of three ships, well escorted by corvettes and destroyers. As we sailed down the Irish Sea the fog suddenly lifted and almost immediately we received an urgent signal from the leading escort: "*Fort Halkett*, there is a floating mine passing close down our port side. Can you see it? You may need to take evasive action."

Luckily it was daylight and clear weather and we saw the mine and I made the minor alteration to pass it safely, some hundred yards to our port side. I said to the artillery rating on watch, "Slip into the chartroom and bring me the rifle there and load it. I'm going to have a pot at that mine." He brought the rifle, but as he handed it to me said, "Almost impossible to hit it with so little to see, bouncing around, and with our ship's movement."

I agreed with him. I was a poor shot, usually missing the targets at fairs, and having no experience with a service rifle. I put it to my shoulder, looked casually along the sight, pulled the trigger – and the mine blew up. I had hit one of the tiny horns which caused it to explode.

The senior escort steamed alongside. The captain shouted over the loudhailer, "Who blew the mine?"

When I answered that I had, he replied, "Bloody good shooting. We had two machine guns and several rifles potting at it; you sink it with a single shot!"

All of us on the bridge burst out laughing. We knew it has been an absolute fluke.

On arriving safely at Southampton I laid out all the Christmas goodies I had brought from New York and invited the customs officers to my cabin. The senior officer whistled and exclaimed, "What have we here? Harrods' food department?" I told him Jim Marjoribanks' request, that if the gifts could not be brought in, at least let them be confiscated and given to someone who needed a better Christmas.

One of the customs men pointed at the lemons and asked jokingly what they were; none had been coming to Britain for years. Then he asked, "Can I have one, please, to auction for charity at our Christmas party? I'll let you know how much we get for it." (Next day he came back and said he'd auctioned it for forty pounds for charity!)

Then the customs men discussed how best to arrange the paper work so that I could bring the gifts ashore. When one picked up some nylon stockings and asked if they were silk, I said, no, they were nylon. I must be mistaken, he replied as he fingered them; there was a very heavy duty on nylon; silk much less. Taking his hint, I said maybe I was mistaken.

So it went with all the items, with far less duty to pay than I had feared. The senior officer gave

me a receipt, saying he didn't know how I would
get everything past the policeman at the dock gate,
but wishing my friends a very happy Christmas.
My fellow officers then helped me repack the gifts;
the second mate had a bright idea – put as much
as you can into the empty chart boxes, he suggested; it would look as though they contained the
old charts which had to be brought to the chart
office for correction. We stashed everything in
except the turkeys, which were too big.

We loaded a taxi and I sat up front with the
driver as the back was full. At the gate we were
stopped and the policeman asked me what I had
in back. I handed him the receipt pink slip.

"I see," he said, "turkeys and stockings – what
else?"

"Christmas presents from friends in America for
their poor starving friends in the UK," I told him.

"And I suppose those are charts going ashore
for correction." I said nothing.

"Carry on," he said. "Happy Christmas!"

I took a lemon from my pocket and offered it
as a memento. He gave a great grin. "My wife will
be tickled pink."

I left the *Fort Halkett* regretfully. She was a good
ship, and I liked and respected Captain Poulsen
and his wry sense of humour. Then I headed off
for leave and a long awaited time with my wife
and daughter.

6

Shorts, santos and scurvy

My leave went by fast, a time of relaxation when I turned my mind off and enjoyed life with Nancy and our young daughter, Sue and visits with friends.

All too soon I set off for Liverpool to join my next ship, the *Gascony*, a small intermediate cargo liner belonging to the Royal Mail Line. That line was one of the prestigious companies that "carried the flag" for Britain. It operated routes between UK and South America's east coast, especially Brazil, Uruguay and Argentina. The big "money-spinning" cargo was chilled meat for the butcher shops of Britain.

Gascony was one of three smaller ships which were not refrigerated, carried no passengers and, in addition to Rio de Janeiro and Buenos Aires, called at smaller ports dotted down the coast of South America. She was not as glamorous as the flag ship *Andes*, but was for me more pleasant and interesting than the big passenger boats.

Before we sailed I was surprised by a visit from

my brother Hannen. The docks were subject to
heavy bombing and were closed to everyone without an official pass. Hannen was in his Army uniform, but dishevelled and dirty. He had come as
one of a gang from Saighton camp, sent to dig out
bodies from bomb shattered buildings. He looked
worn out, emotionally exhausted and in need of
food and rest. We chatted until late in the evening
and he spent the night on the settee in my cabin.

Early next morning, da Silva, my Portuguese
steward, arrived with his customary tray laden
with teapot, milk jug, biscuits and cup and saucer.
He woke me gently and asked, "Does madam take
sugar?" He glanced over at Hannen's tousled hair
protruding from a rug. This woke us both fast,
with much laughter. Hannen asked, "Do you often
have ladies sleeping on your settee?" I was able to
answer truthfully, no.

Da Silva was a treasure – elderly, very formal
and dignified. He took the greatest care of the
officers in his charge. For instance, as I was going
ashore one evening he ran after me, calling "Sir,
sir, you cannot go like that; your shoes are not
clean enough." I answered that it was dark and no
one would see them. "Oh no, sir, suppose someone
noticed them, they would say what a bad steward
this officer has. Please allow me to clean them for
you."

I was flabbergasted. This was the first steward
I'd had who even offered to clean my shoes or
cared two hoots what I looked like. Da Silva, with
all his concern, was never servile; always had dignity and standing in the eyes of all our officers.

Later, we sailed down the Mersey, around the

north of Ireland, picked up a convoy and steamed peacefully to the entrance to the Mediterranean. It was the start of a six month journey out through the Tropics and back during which I came to know my fellow ship's officers very well. Captain Harry Wright was a quiet, neat little man, always in complete control of the situation. Chief officer Bill Ballardie, a burly, red faced, older man, was very experienced, but was believed to have blotted his copy book in some minor way and had been passed over for promotion. He never seemed to go to bed; whenever I called him for night watch I found him fast asleep at his cabin table. He always awoke very alert and capable. I was third mate and my closest friends were "Sparks" the radio officer, and Bob, a senior apprentice, shortly to qualify as third mate. The two were opposites – Sparks was like quicksilver, a Glaswegian, full of life and fun; Bob was ponderous, thoughtful, thorough and reliable.

The outward voyage was smooth and routine, apart from a minor incident. When we reached the tropics the captain issued the order: "From tomorrow morning tropical kit will be worn." I donned the tropical kit I had worn with the lines on which I had served – white shirt with epaulettes, white shorts, socks and shoes. When Captain Wright came on the bridge during my watch he asked where my number tens were. I asked innocently what a number ten was, knowing full well that it was a long legged pair of khaki trousers.

"The kind I'm wearing, of course."

"Sir, I don't have any."

"Then you'll have to get some. Company regulations."

I asked where I could get some.

"When we dock in Rio de Janeiro."

"I'm sorry, sir. I doubt if that's possible. I'm close on six feet five inches; I can't buy clothes off the peg; I doubt if we'll be in Rio long enough to have anything made."

The Captain grunted we would have to see.

We had just two passengers on board, an elderly couple named Harwood, guests of the company. One morning, as we were sailing down the coast of Brazil, a Royal Navy cruiser appeared over the horizon and pulled alongside us. A man dressed only in white shorts, and with a cap with gold braid, climbed up on the bridge superstructure and started signalling with semaphore flags. His message: "Do you have Mr and Mrs Harwood on board?" I signalled back, "Yes." "Could you ask them to come on the bridge? This is their son calling."

The Harwoods were fetched and they had a friendly conversation through me and the semaphore flags. Then the cruiser increased speed and left us.

"Did your son have braid on his cap?" I asked Harwood.

"Yes, he's just been promoted Rear Admiral from Commodore." We all looked at the departing cruiser with awe. At that time Commodore Harwood was our great war hero, having sunk the Germans' most destructive raider, the pocket battleship *Graf Spee*. Later, as we passed Montevideo, we saw the *Graf Spee* sitting on the bottom outside the harbour, where she had been sunk by our three small elderly light cruisers.

As Admiral Harwood's figure disappeared in the distance, Captain Wright turned to me and said with a smile. "Foss, I noticed the Admiral was wearing shorts, and so were his officers. So I suppose shorts are all right for the Royal Mail Line."

Soon afterwards I was fated to cut across another Royal Mail time honored tradition. As third officer I was responsible for cargo loading plans, a complicated affair. We had loaded general cargo – machinery, cotton, all kind of things. These were stowed in compartments in the hold, destined for many ports. Each item had to be documented on a plan – what it was, where it was located, its weight – so that on arrival at each port vehicles could be lined up in proper order to remove the cargo. Time and money would be wasted if this was not done efficiently.

The Royal Mail had an established system: Plans for each hold were drawn up on a sheet, four feet long and two feet wide. On these I had to record the items in approximately the position in which they were stowed, in the colour designated for each port. The big sheet was ungainly to hold and in my "know-it-all" style I went ahead with a better method. I made booklets, with one page allocated to each compartment of the holds, showing the position of each item, and on the opposite page the name of the port destination and list of items. At the front of the booklet was a pull-out layout of the whole ship, giving the overall position of cargo for each port.

When we reached Rio the head stevedore came for the cargo plan and I gave him three copies of my booklet. He was delighted; "This is so much easier to work with than those clumsy old plans," he said. I was feeling pleased with myself at having made a big improvement for the Royal Mail Line, but when the three copies of the booklet required by the Rio office arrived there, they caused an uproar. The manager came aboard in a fury, saying that I was upsetting their routine arrangements and demanded the old style plans. I lost my temper and told him that if he insisted on his old fashioned idea he could work it out himself. Later, I was ashamed of myself because I had put Captain Wright in an awkward position. I think he agreed with my method, but had to support the official company line.

I heard later that the Rio manager had suggested to the captain that I should be dismissed on our return to the UK, and that the captain had smiled and replied, "If indeed we should manage to get back to the UK without being sunk, I doubt if the matter would assume any importance, do you?"

During our lay-over in Rio I managed as usual to see something of that beautiful area. It was my custom always to go everywhere by public transport, which allowed me to see more of the life of ordinary people. One evening, on my way back from visiting friends, I caught a bus, handing over the last of my Brazilian money to pay the fare. It drove to a terminus and I was dumped out, unable to make anyone understand where I wanted to go. I set out walking, lost and nervous. I was on the edge of the Favela district, an area of shacks where thousands of peasant immigrants to the city lived, huddled together, with no sanitation.

I had become really worried, when I saw a small,

bearded man, dressed in a long coat and a broad brimmed hat. I decided he must be a rabbi and, summoning my very restricted Yiddish, I rushed up to him and asked the way. He grinned and said that was where he was going, and escorted me almost as far as my ship. We chatted about England, Brazil, Siberia, where he had come from, and we laughed together. It was a memorable evening, and one of many such unexpected and delightful encounters I made in many parts of the world.

I found the Brazilian people I met very friendly and courteous – even the police. One evening several of us went ashore and, feeling cheerful, began running down one of Rio's boulevards, Avenida Rio Branco, in a line, making rugby passes with a cap. Up roared a police car and we were arrested and taken to a police station, where we were welcomed by the station captain, who told us the police were against the Nazis and wanted Britain to win the war. This was an occasion to celebrate the alliance between the two countries, he went on, and out came the wine. For the next hour we celebrated and then a police car drove us to a good restaurant for dinner.

From Rio we sailed down the coast to Santos, which became famous years later around the world as the home town of the great soccer player, Pele. Even at that time it was a city of close to five million people. Lying ahead of us in the harbour was a German freighter. Brazil was still neutral in the war, even though popular sentiment lay with Britain. Our consulate advised us to avoid the Scandinavian Bar, just outside the port, since it was a hang-out for German crews in the evenings.

Of course, a dozen or so of our crew decided to go there one evening to show the Germans "what's what". A fight broke out, more friendly than fierce, since it's hard for seamen to hate each other, whatever their nationality, but they did some damage to the place and the police arrived to take British and Germans alike off to jail overnight.

Next morning the captain gave me money and sent me off to bail our men out. Outside the police station I encountered the second officer of the German ship on the same mission for his crewmen. As we waited, we sat and talked, he in English and I in German, and we laughed together at the stupidity of our crews. My crew came out first, but when I came to pay the bill I had insufficient money. I was about to send them back and return with more cash, when the German officer said, "Let me lend you some. I have more than enough for my crew." I borrowed the money from him, arranging to pay him back when we got aboard.

We marched our lads back to the docks, keeping on opposite sides of the street. Once aboard I told the captain what had happened; he laughed and handed me the money to repay the German officer, saying, "We may have to kill them later, but we don't have to cheat them." I went aboard the German ship, repaid the money and had a chat with some of the officers and found them all fed up with the "bloody war". Later, I saw their second officer standing on the poop, obviously preparing to sail. I called across to thank him and say goodbye.

Under international law, when enemy ships sailed from the same port, the first one to leave must be given twenty-four hours clear time before the second ship left. The advent of radio had changed the situation, since the first ship could now signal one of its warships with the location and expected departure time of the second ship; our sailing could now be dangerous. As the German ship left, their second officer shouted, "Goodbye, good luck. See you in one of our prison camps!" He shrugged and smiled ruefully. I watched them let go on all their mooring lines but one and thought to myself, well, it could soon be the end of the war for me – a prison camp or the waves. Suddenly I saw the lines being put out again and their second officer called out to me, "We have engine trouble and can't sail."

I rushed up to the captain and told him. He immediately booked the next sailing time, so that we could get ahead of the Germans. As we departed, the German second officer called to me, "Good luck; come and visit me in prison camp in England!" I waved sadly and we left. I later learned that his ship had been sunk by one of our warships on patrol in the South Atlantic. I did not know his name and could not discover whether he drowned or ended up in a British prison camp. Such are the uncertainties of life for a sailor in wartime.

Our next port of call was Curitiba, a little place in those days as delightful as its musical name. It lay not far south of Rio, a long way up a river. The captain took me ashore for a game of snooker in the British Club and from there to call on an elderly Welsh couple. They had come some twenty years before with a British company to build the Leopoldina Railway; the husband was a blaster by

profession and had helped dig the tunnels through
the mountains. Then an explosion had totally
blinded him. Their native South Wales was in the
midst of a deep depression and they had decided
to stay on. They settled in Curitiba, where they
made many friends among the Brazilians. They
entertained us with a fine Welsh tea and I was
uplifted by their courageous spirit, making the
most of their lives out of a tragedy that might have
embittered them.

At the next port, Rio Grande do Sul, the local
branch of the world-wide "Daughters of the
Empire" put on a dance for our whole crew. The
scene was reminiscent of the Palm Court at
Brighton, with potted palm trees, very English furniture and a slow serving bar. A three-piece orchestra, fiddle, piano and drums, soldiered away val-
iantly. Sparks and I had a few desultory dances
and were thinking of moving to more lively entertainment, when through the door came a fascinat-
ingly beautiful girl, wearing a bright red dress with
strapless shoulders and a full skirt.

I reached her first and asked for a dance; the
orchestra broke into a samba and she danced light
as a feather. She spoke little English, but when she
opened her mouth I was enveloped in a waft of
garlic. As soon as the music finished I handed her
over to Sparks, not mentioning the garlic. As soon
as that dance ended, Sparks rushed me out to a
typical Brazilian restaurant opposite, where he
ordered fried chicken cooked in a heap of garlic
for us both.

Back at the dance we took turns dancing with
the lass, enjoying the mutually garlic atmosphere

right to the end, when her husband, an American minesweeper captain, arrived to take her home.

Entering and leaving Rio do Sul requires good judgment. At the entrance to the river the tides have built up a sandbank which can only be passed by a ship of our size during a two-hour period at high tide. We did not complete our cargo reloading until past the top of the tide. The Captain consulted with the pilots and local experts, who assured him there was enough time to cross the bar safely. They were wrong. Our bows were stuck on the sands for about eight hours; fortunately the hull received no damage because we had been steaming slowly.

On our return trip we joined an American coastal convoy off Guantanamo, Cuba. For the first time I saw a dirigible escort – small sausage-shaped balloons equipped with submarine detectors flying ahead of and alongside our convoy. There had been many sinkings along the US coast recently. But a greater danger than enemy submarines on this trip was the erratic shooting by American coastal trading ships. They had had no experience of the war until now, and their trigger-happy firing of their guns when they suspected any danger was a hazard to other ships in the convoy.

The most serious problem for our crew on our voyage home was the deterioration in our food. Wartime shortages and having to spend so much time going out of our way to join convoys and then travel at minimum speed combined to put a strain on our provisioning. Food on all Royal Mail vessels was well cooked and beautifully served, but as we travelled north we ran out of potatoes and noticed that we were being served mutton every day. The steward told me that the ship chandlers he had ordered from in Brazil had been very short of beef, pork and poultry.

Our ship lacked refrigeration space for fresh vegetables for more than one month at sea, and we were having to spend longer periods between ports. We had to make do with dried beans along with the mutton. By the time we reached Halifax we were existing on roast mutton, boiled mutton, fried mutton, minced mutton, mutton prepared every way the cook could devise, and always with beans.

We only reached Halifax in time to join a convoy setting sail – no time to stop and provision, and off we set for another three weeks dawdle across the Atlantic. Each day I could feel myself getting more unwell; my teeth were becoming loose in my gums and my nails in my fingers. I began to bleed slightly from my gums and from cracks in my hands. And I was becoming lethargic. Others in the crew started experiencing the same symptoms.

On arrival in the UK we were ordered to sail up the Manchester Ship Canal and a Royal Mail Line superintendent came aboard to check on the crew. As he stepped off the ladder on to the deck he asked a sailor brightly, "Had a good trip?" The deck hand replied, "Full of bloody beans and mutton. The Germans didn't try to sink us, but the bloody steward tried to murder us with his food."

As soon as the ship tied up in Salford docks someone went ashore to telephone and came back yelling. "Quick everyone, there's a hot potato barrow just outside the gates." Everyone dashed ashore and guzzled every potato on the barrow. Next morning we were all feeling a lot better.

As soon as I had paid off the ship I took a train to London, and because I was still having trouble with my gums and cracked hands I consulted my surgeon friend. Campbell Milligan, who had saved my life when I'd had pneumonia. He sent me on to a skin specialist in Harley Street, who looked me over and said enthusiastically, "My dear chap, I'm so pleased to see you. You've got scurvy. I've never seen it before in my life. I've read about it and wondered what it was really like. May I bring in some students to examine you? It will be a great lesson for them."

He went on to question me in detail and I told him how the crew had been on a lime ration until the lime ran out, and the one thing we ached for was a potato. "Quite right, my boy," he chortled; "Contains masses of vitamin C, best preventative for scurvy." His students examined me; he prescribed vitamin C, and gradually I got better, although for years my teeth and hands gave me trouble.

One evening soon afterwards in London, I was having a meal with an important shipping insurance man and happened to tell him the story of our diet problems on the homeward trip. He asked whether I had informed the Royal Mail Line. I said I had not, since it had not been their fault and anyway, I had now left the line. He insisted that all shipowners should be informed about what had happened and suggested I should write a letter to *Fairplay*, the shipowners' magazine.

Later on, I did write such a letter, but without mentioning the name of the company. Next day I had a phone call from a Mr Robinson, the editor of *Fairplay*, asking me if what I had written was really true. When I told him it was, he asked, "Which company?"

"Royal Mail."

"Do they know about the incident? They are a very responsible company and I'm sure they must have made provision for this sort of thing. Something must have gone wrong. Would you be willing to meet their general manager and tell him about it? He's a good man; I know him well."

I hesitated, not wanting to become involved or get the captain or steward into trouble, but I was keen that such a thing should not happen again. So I agreed. A few days later I was invited to join Mr Robinson for lunch at the Palmerston Restaurant, a more elegant place than I was used to patronising. We were joined by a gentleman whom my host introduced as Mr Barber, general manager of the Royal Mail. Over coffee at the end of a sumptuous meal, Robinson asked Barber whether he'd seen the letter in last month's issue of his magazine about the crew of a British line company getting scurvy.

"I certainly did, and everyone on Leadenhall Street was talking about it and wondering if it was true and if so, which company it was."

"And would you like to know?"

"I certainly would."

Robinson looked at him quizzically; "It was the Royal Mail."

"Impossible!" exploded Barber. "Such a thing couldn't happen to us. We employ a large staff to take care of our catering and are very proud of it."

"Would you like to meet the author of the letter?"

"I would indeed!" declared Barber, with an edge in his voice. Robinson turned to me, "You are the gentleman who wrote the letter, are you not?"

"You!" roared Barber. "Which ship? Who was the captain? Where did she go that trip? What was your position on board?"

I answered all his questions straightforwardly as he took notes. At the end he said very quietly he must get back to the office and look into all this. I started to defend the captain and chief steward, but Robinson stopped me, saying, "Mr Barber is a very fair man. He'll get to the bottom of this and deal with the people who were really responsible."

We went our separate ways and I heard no more of the matter, but later I learned from a friend in the head office of Royal Mail that some very senior heads had rolled.

7

Family crisis

My leave this time was four months, the longest since the outbreak of war. As I look back on those leaves, I regret how little opportunity I had to get to know my daughter. The times I spent with Susie were a surprise and joy, but the intervals between them were long and she grew up without the security of a home as we were always moving between temporary accommodations.

I love children and have always found it easy to get on with them, but during those crucial years between three and ten Susie had little opportunity for real rapport with her father. Somewhere I abdicated the responsibility for getting along with her; we both seemed to have fixed opinions and too often our differences became emotional and reason flew out of the window. Many times on my travels I sat down to write to Susie, filled a page or two, then threw it in the waste basket because I couldn't seem to say what I wanted.

I would like to blame the distance between us on the stresses of my wartime journeys. It is true that I arrived home still tense with the dangers I encountered; I moved from that world of fears and sudden demands to an entirely different atmosphere. But I now see that I was a poor father, swinging too far on that tightrope between discipline and indulgence. And unconsciously I wanted to fashion my daughter in my own image – a grave mistake.

I was asked if I would like to join the *Empire Buckler* as second mate. She was a new ship, built on the north-east coast to wartime standards to be managed by Houlder Brothers, an old established shipping line in the meat trade on the South American run. While the company was part of a conglomerate closely connected with the Royal Mail Line, it had a much more relaxed and informal style of operating its ships. I found this style more profitable than one which emphasised appearances, and in recent times it has become only too clear that without adequate profits companies are out of business and thousands of employees are out of work.

I joined the *Empire Buckler* in London. She was a comfortable ship, although not so well fitted out as the Fort ships built in Canada. The captain was a jolly fellow named Grant, tall, full of life and very competent. Our lives had once crossed in Liverpool when I was standing by the *Tacoma Star* after she had been sunk in the docks next to the *Elstree Grange*, captained by Grant, and I had joined in trying to fight a fire aboard her.

The first mate was a small chap, Stephenson, very clever, but moody as hell, perhaps because he drank too much at times. I served the twelve to four watch, night and afternoon, and Stephenson was supposed to relieve me at four. He was fine at four p.m., but the devil to wake at four a.m. Sometimes I had to go down, pick him out of his bunk and stick him under the shower.

Our trip to Buenos Aires was uneventful, almost like peacetime. The German U-boats were now suffering more losses than our merchant ships. On arrival at Buenos Aires we spent a busy week discharging our cargo and then loading meat, but evenings and weekends were free to go ashore. The attitude of the Argentinians towards the British had changed from the earlier days of the war, when Nazi troops were over-running Western Europe and making deep inroads into the Soviet Union. At that time the British were treated very warily, but as the tides of war began to turn, Argentinians were openly expressing their dislike of the Nazis and sympathy with us. As a result I could roam freely and visited many friends.

One morning, after spending the night aboard as duty officer, I was up early supervising the opening of cargo hatches and setting the stevedores to work, then went to call mate Stephenson to breakfast. He was not in his room, which was unusual, since although sometimes coming back inebriated, he was not a womaniser, staying ashore. I immediately went to see the captain and was startled when his steward told me that the captain also was absent. I was worried, and even more alarmed when the second steward reported that the chief steward was also missing.

It was after ten o'clock, loading was nearly completed and we were due to sail that afternoon. I

left the third mate in charge and took a taxi to
Houlder Brothers' office. They phoned around the
police stations until they located all three men
under lock and key. I took a taxi, paid their fines
and we drove back to the ship. On the way we
were overcome by laughter at their adventures.
They had had a few drinks, headed for the big
showground in the centre of the city and enjoyed
themselves shooting at targets in one of the stalls.
The chief mate had been lucky to win a huge rabbit
doll, whom they had christened "Harvey". Then
they had marched with Harvey down the street,
singing a popular wartime song, "Run, rabbit,
run," and an over-zealous policeman arrested them
for being drunk and disorderly.

We set sail on time that afternoon across the
South Atlantic for Freetown, Sierra Leone, where
we were to join a convoy for the UK. From Freetown the convoy crept north at the usual six knots,
a boring pace made more aggravating by some
bossy little Royal Naval ship telling us how to run
ours. We used to talk about how their commanding officer had probably been a small businessman
while we were safely navigating our freighters
around the world. It was fine late spring weather
and most of us were on deck sunbathing. One
afternoon the senior escort ship made a signal to
the commodore ship, which it relayed to us with
a bevy of flags: Each ship was to make a one
hundred and eighty degree turn to starboard and
head back to Freetown. There was heated specu-
lation on board as to the reason.

We steamed that way all night, only to be told
by another bevy of flags next morning to turn

round again and continue on our original course. Shortly afterwards we were ordered to zig-zag according to a certain pattern, a very dangerous manoeuvre, since there were some thirty ships in four lines of eight abreast, only two ships' lengths apart. Each ship required its own turning circle and turning uniformly at such slow speed was very difficult. The manoeuvre was achieved without accident and the commodore signalled congratulations to all ships.

We zig-zagged all day and then, to our amazement, at dusk we were ordered to turn south once more. We continued this kind of movement for four days. It seemed to us the height of folly, since weaving such a pattern was making it easier, rather than more difficult for U-boats to hit us. And if there were no U-boats around, it was a consummate waste of time and fuel.

We were never told what it was all about, but after the war I met a rear-admiral, who, I discovered, had been commodore of our convoy. He told me that our Navy had positioned two hunter-killer groups of frigates and corvettes in the area because Air Reconnaisance had spotted a wolf-pack of enemy submarines there. Our convoy was being used as decoy until the wolf-pack had been decimated. Then we were permitted to continue for home.

We left the convoy as it passed round the north of Ireland; We were ordered to go round the north of Scotland and down the east coast to London. London had been a closed port for some years; the east coast route had been dubbed "E-boat alley" because the German torpedo boats had made it impossible to use. I believe we were the first freighter, with our precious cargo of meat, to be allowed to use the route, since the war had entered a new phase, with our enemy in retreat.

We had one more scary episode as we were steaming towards the Minches, between the Hebrides Islands and the mainland. A Navy corvette approached, set on a course to come close to our starboard side. Its commanding officer was standing on the wing of the bridge, intent on giving us orders through a megaphone, while his ship was being "conned" by a young RNVR sub-lieutenant. It was obvious to us that unless they reduced speed or altered course hard to starboard they were going to ram us. We yelled at the CO, but he was so engrossed in passing his orders to us that he failed to grasp the situation. They rammed us a glancing blow, but as they were so much smaller and fragile than us they received the major damage. The CO was knocked off his feet and as he staggered up we heard a stream of colourful abuse directed at the little sub-lieutenant.

Our damage was minimal and we proceeded on our way through the Pentland Firth, down the coast and up the Thames to London. What a sight it was to gaze at the old docks, the giant Ford factory at Dagenham, the small pubs and men fishing on the quays. This was a scene I had not glimpsed for four years, unsure whether I would ever see it again. The Royal Docks, where we tied up, looked a little grimier, but the dockers were the same cocky, cheerful crooks, great workers who could turn us around faster than any dockers in the world.

I was to remain on ship as duty officer over the weekend and I phoned Nancy, asking her to bring Susie and join me on the ship for those days. My call sparked the worst crisis of our marriage.

That marriage, begun under tough circumstances, was something for which neither of us had been prepared. I had fallen in love with her, hook, line and sinker, but knew almost nothing of her family and background, which were very different from mine. Hers were well-to-do, her life secure and comfortable. I had been brought up by foster parents and at boarding school, seeing little of my mother, who was busy taking care of a hotel. I knew virtually nothing of family life.

After being married twice in nineteen thirty-six, first in a registry office and then in church, we had our baby very soon and after two years I was off to Germany for six months and before long was off to sea. Our times together from then on had been few and far between. Separation was easier for me than for Nancy. I had the distraction of heavy duties and responsibilities, wartime dangers and constantly changing scenes. Nancy was left alone, working with my mother at the hotel in an unreal atmosphere with guests who were always complaining of wartime privation.

Then she had to move again and found a flat which suited her needs, but when I joined her there on leave it did not seem like home to me – a place Nancy, rather than the two of us, had chosen. By this time we had been married five years, of which we had been apart more than two. We had lived in four homes and had never settled down as most couples do.

When I telephoned Nancy to ask her to join me on the *Empire Buckler* there was a long pause. Then she said, "I can't come to you for the weekend. I have a prior engagement. I didn't know you'd be arriving and this is a long standing arrangement."

"Well, put it off," I replied. "I have only a short time in the country and anyone would understand this is a priority."

"I can't. I made a promise."

I argued, but got nowhere, and she rang off. I went slowly back to the ship, my mind in a whirl. Suspicions, fears and all kinds of wild ideas went rushing through my mind. What could be more important than coming to see me, her husband, who was in the country such a short time? I could be sent overseas again in a few days, perhaps to be killed, and never to see each other again. I was alone on the ship, except for an aged night watchman, and felt as though I was in prison. Back in my cabin I resorted to that source of peace and patience I had found, a quiet time. I felt sure that whatever was wrong, there was an answer if I had faith.

Next morning I had a message from the company office that my wife had phoned and wanted me to call her. I hurried to a phone. When she answered it was obvious that she was in a deeply emotional state. "I had to phone you," she said. "I had to be honest with you. I'm in love with another man. I want a divorce."

I was completely shattered and yet I knew there was hope because there was honesty between us as a bond. The trouble was out in the open.

"Who is he?" I asked.

Nancy said I didn't know him. She had only met him since I'd been away.

"Is that who you were going away with for the weekend?"

"No, not at all. I'm going away with two friends I work with at the Theatre Royal for a break we all need."

I knew that at that time Nancy was working as catering manager for the Women's Voluntary Services at the biggest troop canteen in Bournemouth, in the Theatre Royal. Nancy rang off.

My pride was deeply hurt. How could she care for someone more than for me? I resorted again to a time of quiet during which I had the thought, "And why should she not, poor lass? She has been stuck on her own in Bournemouth; her family is in Bristol; the town has been bombed; she has worked too hard and too long. It's absolutely natural that a young, pretty lass like her should be approached by men. She probably needs their companionship."

But what should I do? As I sat quietly, it became perfectly clear in my mind. I must go to Bournemouth and straighten this thing up. But the trouble was that I was on duty and could not get leave immediately. Then I had a further thought: "That is bunk. Insist that arrangements be made, and go." This proved to be less difficult than I feared.

The captain arrived to make sure the ship was in one piece, not damaged by a V bomb, and I told him I wasn't worried about the ship, but I was about my wife – we were in trouble. I had to go home to see her. He made me tell him the whole story and then agreed to let me go and do the duty himself. I shall always remember him with great gratitude.

I caught a train at Waterloo station. The only other person in the compartment was an Auxiliary Fireman. I must have appeared very grim, because after a while he broke the silence. "You look worried and unhappy. Why don't you tell me about it? We'll never meet again, and once you get it off your chest you'll feel better."

I was startled and felt shy, but the man's openness was encouraging and I was soon telling him everything. When I finished, he responded, "I know one thing you must not do."

I asked him what that was.

"You must not divorce her. Never rush into divorce. I did, and it was the biggest mistake I've made in my whole life. She fell in love with someone else, asked me for a divorce. I consented, and neither of us has been happy since. She married the other man, has five children by him and has to stick with him. We both now know we were too hasty. If you feel you must have a divorce, take a couple of years to make up your mind. It's amazing how things change in that time."

As I was thinking about what he'd said, he added with a big grin, "This man who's after your wife needs tarring and feathering. If you want that done, just call in the fire brigade and we'll take care of it for you!"

When I arrived at the flat I had no key and rang the bell. Nancy came to the door. She was obviously getting ready to go out for the evening. "Oh, it's you," she said. "What do you want?"

"I want to come into my home, if I may."

"Oh well, come in then. I suppose I can't stop you, but I won't be here long. I have an appointment in fifteen minutes."

"That's all right," I said as calmly as I could. "I'm coming with you."

This set her back. "No, you cannot. I have a date. We don't want you there."

I towered above her, telling her she couldn't stop me. "I want to meet this guy who's so much better than I am, see what he's like and whether he's worthy of you and our daughter."

Nancy could do nothing but accept the situation. We headed to the poshest pub in this part of town and in the saloon bar I met this man. He looked presentable, a dentist, married, with two children, but to my eyes a philanderer – but then I was probably prejudiced!

All evening Nancy and he walked from place to place having a few drinks, and I went right along with them, saying very little, but slowly making up my mind what I had to do. When "time" was called at the last pub we headed towards home.

Finally he stopped and said, "This is where I have to leave you for my house," holding out his hand to me, and turning to Nancy, "See you same place tomorrow."

"That you won't," I said quietly, not taking his hand. I added, "You'll never see her again."

"What do you mean? You've been so sensible and civilised, I thought you understood the position."

"I understand the position very well, but you don't. Say a last goodbye to Nancy. If you ever come to see her again, I'll break every bone in your body." I towered over him. "And what's more, I'll break you professionally. People don't approve of dentists having affairs with their patients."

He started to protest that it was not like that, but I stopped him and, moving my face to within inches of his, murmured, "You had better disappear before I half kill you. I mean it."

Back at the flat, Nancy was totally numb and dumb. I went to bed; she went out and was away all night. She told me next morning she had been walking on the cliffs, thinking. I too, had been up very early, trying to be clear what was the right next step.

When Nancy left for work I called on an estate agent and put the flat up for rent. Then I called at the Theatre Royal and asked for an interview with the lady who was my wife's boss. I told her the whole story and asked for her help, saying that I wanted her to dismiss Nancy because I was going to take her to Bristol to her parents. She was very understanding and reluctantly agreed that although she would be lost without Nancy, who was by far her best helper, she agreed that I was doing the best for my wife's future happiness.

Then I went to Susie's school and told the headmistress that this was the last day Susie would be a pupil there as I was taking her to Bristol. And I told her why. The headmistress began to weep quietly; "I am so glad you are doing this. I've watched this thing growing and have been so worried about Susie and Nancy. This man is no good for your wife, but she was so lonely. I am so happy."

I waited until next morning to tell Nancy what I had done and asked her to pack her things as we were catching a train to Bristol around mid-day, and Susie was coming with us. I had phoned the previous evening to my in-laws to let them know we were coming, but not telling them why. The train journey was a nightmare. The three of us were miserable, but I knew I was doing what was right, fighting to save our marriage. It was easier for me than for Nancy and Susie.

When we arrived in Bristol Nancy's parents were of course anxious to know what was wrong. I told them I'd closed the flat and taken Susie out of school and asked if I might leave Nancy and Susie under their care and protection. They willingly agreed, but wanted to know the reason. I knew that I must not tell them, but that Nancy must. I suggested to her father that he should take Nancy into the "morning room" and get her to tell him everything that had been going on in Bourne-mouth. He said that sounded a good idea, and took his daughter off.

My mother-in-law, a cheerful and down-to-earth person, tried to buoy me up while I waited, assuring me how delighted she was to have Nancy and Susie coming to stay. Then Nancy and her father appeared and I insisted that the two of them go back with me to the morning room and made him tell me all that Nancy had told him. He did so, and I said, "That's not everything. Now, please have her tell you *everything*, all the things she could not tell me. It's her only hope for future happiness."

Once again they sat down together for an even

longer period, but when they reappeared Nancy looked less strained. Then I had to leave, first to clear up the flat in Bournemouth, then to get back to the ship. I was shocked at the state of the flat and realised what a miserable time Nancy must have had. She is so neat and tidy, a fanatic about cleanliness. But I found empty bottles and wasted food around, and even a whole rotten ham, tucked away in a cupboard, obviously forgotten. Her friends had taken advantage of her generosity.

As for the dentist, he tried to see Nancy one time when she was staying with a cousin in the country some months later. The cousin, a determined lady, did not like the look of him and warned him off with a shot gun she had on hand in case German paratroopers landed on her farm. That was the last we saw of him. I hope he got over his infatuation and has had a happy marriage with his wife and children. I know very well that what happened to him could very easily have happened to me, had I not had a protective "something" that shielded me and kept me steady and loyal.

I look back on that episode with wonder. I had been given a wisdom far beyond my own.

8

Egyptian eye-opener

Shortly after my encounter with the dentist, when I checked in with our shipowners' pool, I was told that they had established a pool in Alexandria, Egypt, to supply crews for ships arriving there. This was a new development, made possible because German troops had been driven out of North Africa. I was asked to be ready to fly to Alexandria in five days.

I gathered all my sub-tropical gear together and was driven with a dozen others to Lyneham aerodrome in Wiltshire, the big base of RAF Transport Command. There we were fitted out with padded boiler suits, only our hands protruding, each suit equipped with an electric lead for plugging into a socket on the plane to keep us warm. When we boarded a Dakota we discovered why – the plane had no seats or windows, only mattresses on which we were to lie, spread out over the cargo on the floor. The prospect of flying a long distance over enemy territory in these circumstances had little appeal to me.

We sat around on the plane for about half an hour until a general and an admiral suddenly joined us merchant seamen, taking their place on their mattresses. In my ignorance, I resigned myself to a non-stop flight to Egypt, one I calculated would take about twelve hours. But after an hour I felt the plane descending; we landed and the pilot told us we would have dinner and wait until dark for the unescorted flight across the Bay of Biscay, dangerous to fly in daylight.

The general and admiral deplaned and I was about to do so, when ordered to remain aboard. The rest departed in a bus for the terminal. I waited until a car drew up and out jumped an RAF group captain who greeted me warmly and said, "I'm the commanding officer of this station. My wife and I would like you to join us for dinner."

I was flabbergasted. As we drove around the aerodrome towards his house I saw scores of "erks", ordinary airmen, cleaning the place up. "Is all this wash and brush up in honour of a visit of the King?" I quipped.

"Not quite," he smiled. "Your brother will be arriving shortly for dinner with us. It's a good excuse to get the place polished up."

I was astonished. My brother Pat was a group captain, the same rank as my host. Why, I wondered, was he being treated like a VIP? It was explained to me that my brother was the Operations Controller of Transport Command, the eyes and ears of Sir Frederick Bowhill, Air Chief Marshal. As my host described Pat's activities, his standing in my eyes was transformed; I'd always regarded him as an ordinary person of moderate ability, like myself. During the last few years, since both of us had experienced a transformation in our lives, we had become good friends. But now, in this wartime setting, I began to grasp that he was a man of outstanding capacity, making a remarkable contribution towards the winning of the war.*

From the window of my host's house I saw a small plane come in to land and out stepped my brother and he joined us in an excellent dinner. Our time together that evening was the start of a new relationship which I have come to value greatly. It was also an immediate shot of morale in my apprehensive state, setting off for another bout of wartime stresses.

Pat saw us take off for Gibraltar. I climbed on to my mattress and fell fast asleep until our plane's descent into Gibraltar. A VIP wagon took off our "top brass", a mini-bus left with the rest, but again I was told to wait. A car came alongside with a sun-burned group captain, who I later learned was known as "Crackers Carey", because of his dare and drive. He drove me to his home for a swim and breakfast and sightseeing around Gibraltar. He was a good friend of Pat and told me more about my brother's exploits.

Then we were on our way again and as we flew over Tunisia it became uncomfortably hot. All the seamen except me were fast asleep when the second pilot came back to invite me up to the cockpit to watch the desert below, strewn with the

* See *Climbing Turns* by Group Captain Patrick Foss, OBE, published by Linden Hall, 1990

wreckage of the battlefields over which Mont-
gomery and Rommel had fought. We landed at
Castel Benito, a former Italian air base in Libya.
Here once again I was treated to the same hospi-
tality; the CO of the station, Wing Commander
Ogilvie, picked me up, took me to dinner and gave
me a lucid account of the recent fighting in North
Africa. Late in the evening we flew on to Cairo
West, which looked very peaceful under the morn-
ing sunlight.

"Here we go again," I said to myself as the
station CO, Air Commander Whitney Straight,
picked me up in his Rolls Royce and took me to
his office, then on for a sightseeing tour and to the
railway station to catch a train for Alexandria. Pat
had been waving a magic wand on my behalf.

At the station I found that a first class seat had
been booked for me. It was a most impressive
train, superior to anything I'd see back home. It
was beautifully clean, the seats covered with khaki
linen covers which were changed after each journey. With my height I appreciated the extra leg
room. One other seat in the compartment had been
reserved and in due course an officer dressed in
what appeared to be the uniform of a major in the
Egyptian Army arrived. We fell into a conversation
which was so interesting to me that we never did
go to sleep that night.

The officer talked about Egypt's problems – corruption in high places, the frustration he and some
of his friends felt at the condition of his country
and some of the actions he felt were needed to
clear it up. I discovered that he was on his way to
join the guard of King Farouk's palace. I was

greatly drawn to him and admired the depth of his thinking and his grasp of world affairs. When we parted he gave me his card. I barely glanced at it; the name meant nothing to me. Some years later I was going through some name cards I had collected and came upon his: Gamal Abdul Nasser, by then President of his country and famous around the world.

Arrival in Alexandria was something of an anticlimax after all this high living. The Admiralty had commandeered the Grand Majestic Hotel. The lower floors were reserved for Merchant Service ratings and the upper floors for officers, all like myself waiting for ships. I had a luxury room with private bathroom. Its only shortcomings was its bed bugs, before the days of DDT. Twice I had to enlist the help of the Egyptian "chamberman" to remove them. The food was good and suitable for the hot climate.

An elderly naval captain was in command, charged with keeping order among the one hundred merchant seamen sitting around with nothing to occupy their time. One day a delegation of ratings brought a complaint about the food to him. They wanted good old fashioned English food – steak and kidney pudding, steamed duff and the like. The captain cunningly turned to his clerk and asked how many cooks there were among his residents. He was given their names and instructed them to produce what the ratings were asking for. These cooks did not fancy working in the steaming hot kitchen, so they came up with terrible dishes, extra starchy and heavy. Three days later a second delegation came to the captain to ask that the hotel chefs return to do the cooking.

I used my free time to visit as many places and make as many friends as I could. One of the most congenial friends I made was George Yazbak, a soft drink dealer and Syrian Christian, who invited me to accompany him to a "fellahin", a peasant meeting place, way out on the edge of the Sahara desert. I was made welcome; we sat on the floor and were served strong coffee and sweet cakes. George did his best to interpret the fast flow of the conversation in Egyptian-Arabic.

My attention was arrested by a man who had been sitting silently with his back to me suddenly spitting noisily on the ground, rising and making some impassioned statement. George interpreted for me apologetically: "He says he had never before had to sit down to coffee with a heathen dog of an Englishman and he saw no reason for starting now. He was going home, where only good decent Moslems gathered."

"Please call him back," I said to George, "and tell him here is one dog of an Englishman who is humble enough to say he's sorry for our arrogant superiority over the years and wants to learn all that Egypt and the Moslem faith can teach him."

George ran after the man and told him what I'd said. The man stopped, looked around and came slowly back and sat down. I asked George to get him to tell me where we had gone wrong.

Abdul, for that was his name, stared at me. "You are so proud," he said. "Your empire stretches around the world. You say you lead the world, and what do we have? World war. We used

to live that way in the time of the Pharoahs. But
we haven't done that for a thousand years. Who
is more civilised – you or us? You think you are
so clever. I hear you are a navigator. Whose figures
do you clever navigators use? Ours. A thousand
years before any man in Britain could read or write
we invented navigation. Yet you think of us as
illiterate idiots and yourselves as the great know-
alls. Do you want me to go on?"

"Yes, please. I had no idea of these things. I've
always thought that we were the great world
leaders and that Egypt was only partly civilised. I
apologise. I was completely wrong and I ask your
forgiveness."

For the next four hours I learned more about
life and reality from Abdul and his friends than
I'd ever heard before. I began to understand the
bitterness many Egyptians felt towards us British,
and when I was in Algeria, the way the Algerians
felt about the French, who had dominated their
country. It was a great experience and served me
well in the years ahead. So often we seamen only
see the glamorous and the sleazy sides of ports and
countries. In Egypt I had the opportunity to meet
men and women who gave me an appreciation of
the best of their nation.

One morning we woke up to great excitement
outside our hotel in Mohammed Ali Square.
Tanks, armoured cars and troops were massed
there, ready, we were told, to launch an assault on
a building close by, which had been loaned to
Greek refugees. The building had been taken over
during the night by EOKA, the organisation of
left wing Greek revolutionaries, who refused to

surrender it unless the Allies guaranteed that EOKA would be allowed control of Greece as soon as it was liberated from the Germans. It was a delicate issue for the British since the majority of Greeks were opposed to EOKA. It was decided to parley with the EOKA while the military stood by. Eventually an unarmed lieutenant commander was allowed to enter the building. I was told that he was successful in his negotiations; at any rate, the building was opened up and the military force dispersed.

A few days later I was invited to a dance at the Greek Embassy, a very up-class affair. During the evening I noticed a very pretty and charmingly dressed girl sitting by herself. No one seemed to want to dance with her, so I crossed the ballroom and asked her for a dance. It was fun and I joined her at a table with two older people. A few minutes later a lieutenant in naval uniform came up to me and asked to speak to me privately. We walked over to a quiet place and he said, "I am from Security. It is unwise for you to dance with that young lady. She is the daughter of the ex-Shah of Persia, who has been interned as an ally of the Germans."

"So what? I'm not giving her any secrets."

"Of course not, but it can do you no good to be seen associating with the enemy."

I laughed, thinking of the time in Santos with the officer of the German ship and my visit to the German-owned restaurant in Buenos Aires. I had one more dance with the girl. She asked me if I'd been warned off and I told her I had. She said, "The joke is that I'm engaged to a British naval officer. But we'd better not dance together any more. It seems to worry some of the old stuffed shirts."

At last the good ship *Caduceus* arrived, needing a second mate. She was an old north-east coast tramp ship owned by Hall Brothers, a firm noted for its primitive ships, run on a shoestring for several generations. Until now I had only sailed in classy liner companies. I soon learned the difference. The captain, Ronnie Seaborne, was in his early twenties and had just got his master's ticket. The mate was Burns, an ex-policeman, aged twenty-seven. I was second mate, aged twenty-eight, and the third mate, known as "Bloxham", where he had been to school, was thirty-eight and had no ticket of any kind.

Caduceus was an coal burner with no running water in the cabins; if you needed hot water you had to fill a bucket on the focsle, take it to the galley and put it on the stove to heat, for tea, to wash, or whatever. There were four Arab firemen and one Indian. Two Arabs stoked the boilers on the twelve-to-four and eight-to-twelve watches; the single Indian stoked the four-to-eight watches. Only on the Indian's watches did we get full steam He, Alimudden Sayadaruddin, was an artist as a stoker. He told me how he was able to produce twice as much steam as the others; his secret was to put on one small shovel-full every minute, keeping the furnace blazing all the time.

Caduceus had discharged her cargo at Alex, so we sailed "light ship" bound for Takoradi, in what is now Ghana to load bauxite, the ore from which aluminium is made. What a relief it was to be able to steam the length of the Mediterranean free from fear of attacks by Italian naval ships and with little danger from the air, since the Allies had gained control of all the airfields in North Africa. We ambled down the West African coast at our full light ship speed, a magnificent seven knots! A couple of anxious days passing through the Dakar area went by uneventfully. Around Dakar German submarine wolf packs had been attacking Allied shipping, but we figured it unlikely that a submarine would risk revealing its position for the sake of sinking an old rust bucket carrying no cargo.

Loading of ore cargoes is a boring job. We tied up under huge tips and the ore in the form of rocky dirt came in on moving belts and poured into the holds. All our officers had to do was to watch that the ore load was balanced in each hold so that there was no danger of *Caduceus* breaking her back, and that we reached the maximum load without sinking below the legal load line. When the day's work was done we spent the evenings up town in a bar and enjoyed meeting with some of Takoradi's cheerful people. But during our stay we encountered a crisis.

As we returned to the dock one night we found cars with civil and military police and a great air of excitement. We learned that a Royal Naval petty officer on a small minesweeper docked in the port had been returning to his ship in an intoxicated state when a Hausa policeman at the dock gate had asked to see his pass. The story being circulated was that the petty officer had snarled, "I show no passes to bloody niggers. Let me through or I'll beat you up."

The policeman had stood his ground; the officer had shoved; the policeman had started to restrain him physically and the officer pulled out a knife and plunged it into the policeman's chest. He fell to the ground and the officer passed by, shouting an insult, and boarded his ship, remembering nothing of the incident when he woke next morning, it was said.

A wave of fierce anger swept across Ghana as Africans waited to see whether the petty officer would be brought to trial. The Hausas were a desert tribe, with a fine physique and bearing, well suited for the police force, although known to be sometimes over strict in enforcing the law. In those days many whites in Africa were still living in their world of racial superiority, assuming they could treat blacks harshly to maintain order and discipline. It was a dangerous situation which could easily escalate into violence. We sailed before the issue was resolved, but I believe that in the end the petty officer stood trial and was given a short sentence in prison.

We sailed for Birkenhead, calling at Freetown, Sierra Leone, where we joined a convoy. My chief memories of Freetown are of a magnificent beach, rivalling anything to be found in Australia or Florida, and of superb cream cakes supplied at the YMCA, baked by Italian prisoners of war. In Freetown I also had to visit a coal dump to negotiate the purchase of bunker fuel for our ship. I located the manager, a Norwegian, in his wooden shanty atop the huge coal dump, some forty feet high and one hundred yards long. I climbed wooden steps and knocked on the door of the hut.

It opened, to reveal not only the manager but a full grown leopard standing alongside him. I jumped backwards, scared out of my wits.

"Oh, hello," said the manager, "Come in and have a drink."

"First, would you kindly tie up that brute."

"Oh, don't worry about him. He's lived with me since he was a few days old. He won't hurt anybody."

I objected that he might know that, but I didn't, and wasn't sure that the animal did. And I couldn't talk business with it around. So the manager took the leopard into another room and shut the door.

"Aren't you afraid he'll revert to his jungle habits?"

"It's possible, but he's shown no sign of it yet. As long as I feed and care for him he thinks I'm his mother."

Later, I heard the leopard had attacked him and had to be shot.

The *Caduceus*, now heavily laden, set off in the convoy, but had difficulty in keeping up with its six knot speed. The convoy commodore signalled us to keep our station as we were endangering the convoy's safety and added that if we could not maintain station we might have to be left behind – and there were reports of a wolf pack operating in those waters.

Next day our chief engineer came to the bridge and said to the captain, "We will have to stop. I have a leak in one of our boilers. We'll have to put it out and retube it as soon as it's cold."

Caduceus slowed to a halt and lay still in the water. The convoy continued on its way. For three days our ship wallowed in the eerie silence, with no steam to operate any of our machinery. All the engine room crew and some us as volunteers worked as long as we could stay awake to finish the temporary repairs. There was tenseness all through the crew as we sat there defenseless, and nearly everyone was making silly little jokes at which we laughed. I think the only one of us who showed no fear was the little old Hindu fireman, Sayadaruddin. He seemed to accept everything cheerfully as "fate". The captain, full of youth and energy, worked without any rest, but he was as obviously worried as anyone.

We eventually hobbled on at about four knots to Gibraltar, where we put in for repairs. There, consuming considerable amounts of alcohol in the bars, some of the crew found release from their tension. Those of us who enjoyed dancing were disappointed to find no women on the Rock at that time, except for players in the bands. Since I could perform a little on the drums I took the place of the lady drummer to free her to dance with my friends.

One evening, as some of our crew returned to the ship they came on stoker Sayadaruddin lying in the gutter, beaten up. They got him into a hospital. He was returned to the ship in due course, covered in bandages, but insisted on keeping his watch and did so after six days, when we sailed, sufficiently repaired to join a convoy heading for the UK.

Meantime, however, there had been a tense incident when some of our crew decided that Sayadaruddin had been attacked by the crew of a South

African minesweeper docked close to us. With no evidence to support their belief, a gang armed with crowbars and pickaxes set off in the small hours to board the minesweeper. To reach her they had to creep across the deck of a British destroyer. They reached the South African ship and started to smash up its mess room. When the noise roused its crew our men rushed back across the destroyer to safety. It was my night on board looking after the ship, and it was I who was disturbed by Navy Police when they came aboard to search for culprits. They found nothing suspicious. I only learned all that had happened after we sailed.

The rest of the voyage home was peaceful except for an encounter with a Fokker Wolff Condor spotter planes circling above us beyond anti-aircraft range. Our anti-aircraft weapon was a laugh. We had a steam pipe attached to the main boilers. To fire at an enemy craft one of us would reach for a mills bomb – the kind used for hand throwing in the trenches, pull out the safety pin, drop it into the steam pipe and turn the tap sharply. The steam pressure hurled the bomb into the air. It had to be timed exactly in order to explode in front of the plane, a virtual impossibility, at least for us, although we did hear of it working with others on a few occasions.

We docked in Birkenhead on an overcast drizzly day. The crew was paid off and sent home, leaving a shore night watchman, the captain, mate and myself to cover the ship. Discharging our cargo took a week, then permanent repairs could begin. Supervising unloading was an easy task – watching the great grabs picking some five tons of bauxite at a time and dumping it in barges. The mate and I slept each night on board. The night after discharging was completed, while the *Caduceus* was lying waiting for a repair berth, a storm broke out.

About two a.m. we were woken by a loud report which the mate and I recognised to be the parting of one of our mooring ropes under the strain of the violent wind. The mate sent me on to the quay to take out another line and make it fast. This was no easy task for two men; the line was stiff fibre rope, seven inches in diameter, maybe one hundred feet long. As we were wrestling it we heard a line part at the other end of the ship and within five minutes all the lines had gone. The *Caduceus* was being blown down the large Bidstone pool, totally out of control, five thousand tons of ship bouncing around like a pingpong ball.

It takes at least twelve hours to get up steam in the boilers and our boilers were lying in pieces, waiting for repair. I ran down the dock as the ship was being blown broadside along it. Burns, the mate, kept trying to throw a heaving line to me to haul a mooring line ashore. It was impossible and eventually he gave up.

Amazingly, the *Caduceus* did not hit any of the ships moored on each side of the basin, but ended up at the lower end, blown hard against the dock entrance. The lock remained out of action until the storm abated enough for two tugs to push the *Caduceus* out far enough to get into the basin themselves, make fast to her and tow her back to her berth. There Burns and I made her fast again, this time a lot more securely. Then the two of us

were paid off and set off for home for a badly
needed rest.

9

Close calls and a convict crew

My leave was a short one and I saw little of Nancy and Susie. My in-laws had offered to take care of Susie for a while, leaving Nancy free to take on a new job. She was working in Newbury as catering manager for the American Red Cross at a big club run for the many GIs who were stationed in the area awaiting the Normandy invasion.

I was soon asked to return to Canada to join a ship being built for the Royal Navy, to be manned by a Merchant Service crew and managed by British India Shipping, one of Britain's prestigious companies at that time. To qualify for the job I was told I had to take a course on Gyro at the Sperry factory outside London on the Great West Road. A fellow student on the course was "Jock" Stanley, who would serve with me as first mate. He was a sixty-seven years old, called back from retirement for the war, and found himself totally unable to keep up with his classmates, who averaged around twenty-five.

I did my best to tutor him between classes; I'd

learned some of the basic principles at Pangbourne. Jock gave up any hope of passing, but at the exam he sat next to me and I passed my sheets to him to copy. At my oral test the examiner looked at me quizzically and said, "It's very strange that you and Mr Stanley's papers are identical. I wonder how that happened." I said nothing and carried it no further. We both received our certificates.

On arrival in Glasgow we boarded the *Aquitania*, a Queen of the Atlantic along with her sister ship *Mauritania*, before *Queen Mary* was built. In peacetime she had carried more than one thousand passengers, now she had nearly ten times that number. The ship was full of American airmen heading home on leave. Most of them wore leather anoraks, decorated on the back with scantily clad girls. Sitting ahead of me at the Sunday service they provided an unusual setting for the earnest sermon proclaimed by a Salvation Army officer.

Another feature of the voyage was a non-stop poker game at which a large number of GIs were using the English money which they could no longer use in the States. An American merchant seaman asked if I would lend him ten shillings with which to join the game, promising to repay me with ten pounds. In New York he kept his promise, saying the GIs knew little how to play – he had made several hundred pounds.

From New York I took the train to Montreal, sharing a compartment with the captain of a Canadian ship which had recently been sunk off the coast of North Carolina. He seemed exhausted, rolled into the upper berth and fell asleep. Around two am the door burst open and several drunken

Canadian seamen stormed in, pulled open the cur-
tains of my berth and yanked me out. They seemed
about to beat me up, when one of them yelled,
"Hey, that's not our captain," and asked me where
he was. I assumed they were looking for the man
on the upper berth, but managed to usher them
out and quiet them down enough to find out why
they were angry at their captain. They were drunk
and clearly letting off steam after their torpedoing.
They had a long story to tell about the captain's
behaviour when the ship sank, but next morning,
sobered up, they seemed on good terms with him.

In Montreal I learned more about the ship I was
joining. The *Fort Wrangell* was now half built in
Vancouver, one of a series of special supply ships
for the Navy. After a few days I set off once more
by train across Canada. At Banff, in the Rockies,
we stopped long enough to stretch our legs amidst
snowy scenes. One of the new crew's officers who
was travelling with me was an Australian, Fox-
croft. As he gazed around he called to me, "What's
all this white stuff?" I thought he was kidding, but
he'd not only never seen snow before, but had
never heard of it. He went as crazy as a little kid,
rolling around in it and joining us in a snowball
fight.

In Vancouver our crew got to know each other
as we awaited the completion of our ship. Captain
"Buster", whom I came to know and respect, was
at that moment facing a difficult situation; he had
spent the last seventeen years in command of a
small vessel running round the Indian coast with
Indian officers and crews. This was his first time
in Canada, in charge of a far larger ship, with a

strange crew. He was now pottering around, talking with experts, obviously out of his depth.

As usual, when off duty I enjoyed visiting friends in the city, and this time in Vancouver I had undertaken a special mission. Back in England I had been invited to attend the annual conference of the Trades Union Congress meeting in Blackpool. It was the time of big debate about the opening of a second front on the mainland of Europe. The Communists and left wing were pushing hard for it in order to relieve the pressure of the Germans on the Soviet front. Arthur Horner, Secretary of the Miners' Union, a Communist, spoke in favour of it for one hour. But it was the Secretary of the Seamens' Union, Charlie Jarman, who stole his thunder. He stood up and said, "Talk about a second front, to my members it's all a bloody front." And sat down.

Afterwards I congratulated him on his speech and we became friends. When he heard I was going to Vancouver he came to see me. He asked if I would call on his mother and half-sister, who lived there. His step-father had just died, his mother was very ill and his half-sister was having a hard time with the burden of clearing up the home and making many arrangements. When I arrived in town I found the mother had also died, leaving the sister in a very unhappy state. During the next two weeks I spent my off-duty time helping square things up and giving her some comfort.

As soon as *Fort Wrangell* was completed she moved out of the dockyard to a quay to begin loading stores for the fleet. The ship had five hatches, divided into twenty-six refrigerating compartments to carry food, medicines and other items. She had a large rum locker and a huge NAAFI "goodies" department. We also stored wines, spirits, beers, cigarettes and chocolates in a compartment fitted out with extra heavy locks. In fact, we carried all the stores necessary for feeding a fleet at sea. Our official designation was a Victualling Stores Issuing Ship (VSIS), a new phenomenon – a merchant fleet auxiliary. We also acquired a lieutenant commander who served as a victualling officer. He was a quiet, efficient man who had managed a big victualling depot. Later we acquired a surgeon lieutenant commander, a Canadian named Manning on loan from the Army, to be in charge of the medical stores.

As soon as loading was completed the dock was suddenly cleared of all personnel and, to my surprise, I saw a force of Canadian Mounted Police arrive. They formed a guard along the quay as a train pulled up alongside us. From it streamed a motley gang of men who were to form our crew. They were a "runner" crew from Vancouver enlisted to man *Fort Wrangell* as far as Sydney, Australia. Once there, we were told, British Indian Lascar seamen would take over. This runner crew had just been released from jail for this assignment by the Canadian government, who were, it seemed, delighted to get them out of the country. I could see that Captain "Buster" was worried stiff. This was not only his first white crew, but he assumed it was also a bunch of thugs.

Just before we sailed we received an urgent message to hold for two navy wives, each with a child, who required immediate passage to Australia.

Since we had two cabins available, each with two bunks, we were requested to carry them. The introduction of women into an all male ship's company will cause a stir at any time, since it involves dress, language and deportment. It seemed to our captain – and to me – that it was downright hazardous, with our jail crew. There was no way, however, that the women could be turned down.

They proved to be very different from each other; one was in her early forties, with a ten-year-old son, wife of a naval captain. She seemed very conscious of his rank, rather prissy and very protective of her child. She was very conscious of our unusual crew and appeared to be nervous.

The other young woman was in her early twenties, her son Bobby eighteen months, her husband a newly recruited stores manager, rank of lieutenant commander. She was attractive and sexy and seemed to take the ship's company in her stride. She had the unnerving habit of wandering around the blacked out decks at night, wafting the scent of "Soir de Paris" perfume and quietly singing "Claire de Lune". She may not have realised that all over the ship young men were posted on look out with nothing to occupy their minds.

One evening I decided I had better make clear to her her devastating impact on the crew. I discovered that Joy was a very decent, newly married young woman, in love with her husband and innocent of any idea of complicating the lives of men on shipboard. But as we chatted in her small cabin, Bobby asleep in the top bunk, she sitting on the lower one, and I on the tiny settee, I found myself becoming uncomfortably aware of her charms.

After a while I said I must go; she thanked me warmly for coming; I got up, leaned over and gave her a kiss, which she returned warmly. It was a moment of crisis for me. I am glad to say that I took a quick look at my commitments – to Nancy, to Sue, to my faithful friends and my shipmates – and walked quietly out of the room.

From then on we were good friends. I often looked after Bobby – I have always enjoyed kids. From time to time I caught myself becoming jealous of Joy's friendship with other officers, but I also had a comrade who could supply me with excellent corrective. Surgeon commander Manning was a fat little man with a huge heart. One time when I was starting to pay Joy too much attention I came into my cabin to find, standing on my desk a medicine bottle with a label, "Lydia Pinkham's Pink Pills for Ladies – Two pills to be taken every time you find you are being overtaken by lust."

"Doc" made no comment, even when I thanked him. He just cocked his head to one side, grinned and walked away.

Soon after sailing from Vancouver we were enveloped in thick fog. I was delegated to stand by "Smokey", our inexperienced young radio operator, to help study and plot our radio bearings. Captain was stumping up and down the bridge, smoking one cigarette after another; the chief officer spent his time making up a roster of the crews for lifeboats to be used in case of emergency; the third officer kept checking and rechecking the lifeboats' gear, in case Smokey and I made a mistake and landed us on the rocks. It was an enormous relief when the fog at last lifted.

But I was given no rest; it was my duty to prepare crew lists for the authorities in Wilmington,
our next port of call. Since so many of them had
criminal records, which had to be recorded in case
any of them tried to jump ship, I was kept very
busy, when not on bridge watch twice a day.

When we reached Wilmington, a busy port on
the edge of Los Angeles, my duties were still not
over. I was ordered to report the ship's arrival and
hand over all documents, including the crew lists
to Naval Control. To reach the office I had to walk
some two miles through the docks. I was dressed
in my tropical uniform, cap, epaulettes, white shirt
and shorts. The American sailors and dock
workers had apparently never seen such an outfit
and as I walked by was greeted with shouts, cheers
and remarks like, "Hello, little boy, aren't your
knees cold?"

Once I reached Naval Control the US naval captain quickly glanced through my crew list and
turned to something much more on his mind.
"How many years bridge service have the officers
on your ship had?" he asked.

I did some mental arithmetic and answered that
our five officers had accumulated about seventy
years.

"We are desperately short of watchkeeping
officers," he said. "I think I'll hold your ship up
and have your officers give our pursers and engineers training on deck watchkeeping – everything
from navigation to anchoring."

I was thunderstruck, but noticing the twinkle in
his eye, realised he was joking. Nevertheless, his
problem was a very real one.

Then I remembered that Frank Buchman, whom I had last seen at the conference on Mackinac Island, was staying with friends in Los Angeles and on an impulse telephoned him. When he came on the line he wanted to know where I was coming from and where I was headed. He invited me to visit, but I had to tell him I could not leave ship. When I told him we were bound for Australia he was very interested.

"That's an answer to prayer," he said. "There are three people down there with whom I have been in correspondence for years, but have not had the opportunity to meet. I want you to take them a personal message. They are interested especially in basic things like how to listen to God. I'd like you to call on them and tell them your experience."

Buchman gave me their names and addresses, one in Sydney, one in Canberra and one in Melbourne. Then he added, "Now Denis, when you meet them, don't try telling them a lot about Moral Re-Armament. Just tell them what you know about listening to God. Thank you for phoning. I'll be praying for you on your voyage."

This conversation somehow affected my whole attitude towards this trip. Here I was, in a shipful of criminals, navigating our way through waters unknown to me and threatened by Japanese submarines, worried about Nancy and Susie living amidst the perils from V1 and V2 bombs, and tempted by a delightful young woman. Now I was suddenly entrusted with a mission by a man who seemed convinced that I could deliver a significant message to people who needed it. As I thought about all this on my watch in the early hours I looked up into a serene star-studded sky. A thought dawned: "You are so worried about your family and about yourself. What about all the people around you on this ship?"

Immediately there came to my mind a fellow on board who I knew was very worried about trouble at home. Concern for him and how I might be of some help to him redirected my worries about Nancy and Sue. I also became more closely involved with personnel problems on board. I sat down to breakfast one morning after my early watch and a saloon steward came over to my table and said in his usual surly voice: "Watchyer want?" I answered him very politely, as I usually do to a surly person, "I'll have a kipper, please."

He yelled across the room, "One Jack-the-Ripper for the so-called second officer."

It was not the first time I'd heard him being stupidly cheeky to officers, taking advantage of his being only a temporary steward, and also having a large physique. I thought a moment, then got up, went over to him and said, "Get out of the saloon and send someone else in. And don't come back until you're prepared to apologise and do your job properly."

He turned to me and said, "And who's a brave boy, then?" I answered, "I'm bigger than you and if you don't leave I'll throw you out."

"You wouldn't dare touch me. I'd tell the union; you're all mouth."

I stepped forward, spun him round, took him by the seat of his pants and the scruff of his neck and propelled him out of the saloon. He was shouting to the officers, "You saw that; I'll get you as witnesses when I report this b. . . . to the captain!"

The lieutenant in charge of NAAFI stores, who had been watching with interest, said loudly, "We none of us saw anything unusual, did we?" There was a chorus from the officers, "Nothing at all."

I sent for the chief steward and told him what I'd done. He looked worried, but said, "All right; we'll see what happens."

An hour later, there was a knock on my cabin door. I was startled when the steward whom I had ejected walked in. He said, "I've come to apologise. I made a fool of myself. I am sorry."

I couldn't help smiling as I said, "Good on you, mate. Sit down, have a cigarette and tell me what you were in prison for."

He did. From that time on we were good friends, and he became a reasonably good saloon steward. But he was typical of the crew, who were niggling, unwilling to work, complaining that they were merely a delivery crew and that it was not their job to keep the ship clean. Uppermost in all their minds, of course, was what their fate would be when they were returned to the UK with their prison records.

I was thinking about this situation on the ship one morning as I sat in my cabin. Was there some way we could put an end to all the petty trouble making and improve the atmosphere on board for the rest of the long voyage to Australia. Into my thoughts popped the figure of an able bodied seaman named Rose. He was unusually quiet, clean, nicely mannered, and yet there was something about him which didn't quite ring true. On the spur of the moment I sent a message to him, asking him to see me in my cabin. It was a Sunday morning and he would be free of work.

He came in and I asked him to sit down. "Rose, you interest me very much. You're a very good AB; I wonder why you came to us with a bunch of criminals the Canadians were hurrying out of the country. What were you in prison for?"

He looked at me intently, then asked, "Why do you want to know?"

"I've been wondering whether you were a political prisoner who was jailed as a trouble maker. We are having nothing but problems with this crew – except for yourself. You are obviously the smartest cookie in the crowd and it has occurred to me that you might just be the one who is suggesting all the difficulties we are having."

There was a pause as Rose smiled, then asked softly, "And if that were so, what would you do about it?"

I smiled back and said, "That's easy. I'd ask you to lay off until we got to Australia and you left the ship. We could have a happy and clean ship for the rest of the trip."

"And what would you tell the authorities in Australia about me?"

I thought for a moment and replied, "I doubt if they would ever ask a second mate about anything; if they did I would tell them what I think."

Rose smiled once more. "That's good enough for me."

We shook hands. We had no more trouble that trip.

The story has a sequel. After the war I came

across a photo of Rose in a newspaper article about strikes and a near riot in the port of Avonmouth over Canadian ships. The secretary of the local labour union declared there was a Canadian who was stirring up the unrest on our docks to further his political ambitions in Canada. In the photo, beside the figure of the rabble rouser stood my friend Rose. Later, I learned that Rose had deserted in Canada from a Russian ship, and had lain low for a long time as a "sleeper" before starting up discontent.

Our delightful trip across the Pacific was broken by one scary event. Our route took us on a great curve across the ocean to a control point through which all shipping had to pass, the narrow straits between the islands of Funafuti and Nukufutau. The open voyage of three thousand miles had to focus on these islands. There was no problem with the stellar navigation we used, providing we had clear skies and horizons, and we had these until two days before we reached the islands. Then continuous overcast skies and heavy rain arrived to make navigation very difficult.

We were due to reach the islands about two a.m. and because of wartime regulations all shore lights were reduced. The islands were about three miles apart, flanked by low coral atolls. We had been ordered not to go either to north or south of the islands because of minefields. Visibility was two miles; there was no moon. The captain and I were on the bridge. He seemed unconcerned; I was very uneasy. He seemed to trust my navigation more than I did. He went on chatting away about his time on the Indian coast. There were two lookouts besides ourselves. We were steaming at fourteen knots and according to my calculations we should reach the islands in five minutes, when Joy Cook arrived on the bridge wearing a filmy nightgown and robe. I had jokingly told her that Polynesian natives would come on board from the islands selling souvenirs and she had believed me. Before I could disillusion her the helmsman yelled, "Sir, the gyro compass has gone wrong; it's going round in circles. I have nothing to steer by."

I shot into the wheelhouse and switched over to the emergency magnetic compass, checked the error, then shot out again and searched for some sign of an island. Suddenly we were hit by a tropical rainstorm, reducing visibility to a hundred yards. I stood with my stop watch, calculating when we should be abeam the islands, at which point we needed to alter course by some twenty degrees to port. At this crucial moment I glanced over at the wing of the bridge. There stood Joy, soaked to the skin, her nightclothes clinging to her so tightly she looked in that half light as though she were in the nude. I turned to the captain, "Look on the starboard wing, Sir." He did so and said with a laugh, "As if we didn't have enough distractions!"

At that moment the port lookout called, "I can see an island on the beam, sir."

The starboard lookout shouted, "Island on the starboard beam, Sir."

I looked at the time marked on the chart for a course alteration. My calculations had proved correct, and no one was more surprised than myself – and the captain. We never discussed the point; we were just mighty relieved we had sailed through safely.

10

Australia – land of surprises

We steamed slowly into Sydney Harbour on a
beautiful spring day. It was a Sunday and many
yachts were out, driven by a strong wind, their
crews leaning to windward to keep their vessels
from tipping over. Around them was a flock of
motor launches and ferries. It was a fascinating
sight, with the great harbour bridge looming above
the traffic. I had last seen the famous bridge when
I was sixteen and it had made an unforgettable
impression on me.

We lay at anchor for a couple of days awaiting
our Indian crew, which was due to take over from
our runner crew. As I watched our crew leaving,
packed on to a tug, I realised that I'd become fond
of many of them. Prison records or not, many were
decent enough. As I watched Rose, the under-cover
Communist, departing, I thought to myself that
his undeviating loyalty to his ideology had been a
challenge to my own often pale and puny following
of my Christian faith. There was nothing, I felt,
that he tolerated unless it conformed to his prin-

ciples; he would lie, cheat, even kill for his revolutionary cause. To hate, I decided, was a lot easier than to love.

The Indian crew numbering nearly one hundred arrived in another tug. In charge of them was a "Serang", a headman who personally selected and controlled them. He had arrived aboard earlier, looked over our crew and ship and had refused to bring his men aboard until our jail birds had departed. He was a magnificent big fellow in his early sixties. He toured the ship with the first officer, shook his head and asked for buckets and scrubbing brushes to be issued to his men. The whole vessel must be scrubbed from stem to stern and from top to bottom before his men could settle in. As soon as everything was spotless his men were allowed to move to their quarters.

The deck and engineering crew had all come from Chittagong, in what is now Bangladesh; they were devout Moslems. The cooks and stewards were Christian Catholics from Goa. At first I found them all irritatingly slow and deliberate, although taking pride in the quality of their work. Within hours the standards of service and food moved from the no-star of the previous crew to five-star.

For the journey to Australia we had used only inexpensive silver for our meals. When the Goanese butler came for the good silver the locked cupboard in which it had been kept was opened – and found to be empty. One of the departed crew had stolen everything. It took a few days to obtain replacements but in the end we lived like kings, with five courses to every meal, a remarkable change from the austerities of Britain.

One of the delicacies our cooks came up with was an Oriental curry. Many were the visitors, senior military officers and civilians, who came to savour that dish aboard *Fort Wrangell*. I asked the head cook to teach me how to make his curries; his lessons have stood me in good stead to this day.

Our ship was moved to Little Sirius Cove, a pretty little inlet on the north shore, and we tied up alongside dolphins, pylons driven into the bottom of the harbour in small groups, so that the ship would be secure, with no need to keep anchor watches on the bridge. Once there, we had no idea what we were supposed to be doing. There were very few naval ships in port, so there was little call for victualling. As a result, I had the opportunity to visit friends ashore. One family especially made me welcome in their home, with a bunk on the patio in which to spend my nights.

One morning I remembered the three people whom Frank Buchman had asked me to meet. One of them, Mrs Peggy Wakehurst, lived in Sydney. I rang her number and a very English male voice answered, "The Governor's residence." I thought I had the wrong number, but asked, "Is Mrs Peggy Wakehurst there?" There was a brief silence, then the answer came back, "Ahem, *Lady* Wakehurst is resting. May I give her a message?"

After some hesitation I said, "Yes, please. Will you tell her I have just come from Los Angeles, where I spoke with her friend Dr Buchman. He asked me to contact her."

"One minute, Sir." And I held the phone until

another voice came on: "Oh, hallo, Frank. Are you in Sydney? Welcome."

I explained to Lady Wakehurst that I was not Buchman, but a friend.

"Can you come to tea tomorrow at four o'clock, Mr Foss?"

I thanked her very much and asked how I could reach her address.

"Just ask for Government House. Anyone will tell you how to get here."

I hung up, a little shaken, and next afternoon took a taxi to Government House. From the gates I walked up a long drive to an imposing house, where the butler with the superior voice ushered me into an imposing sitting room. Lady Wakehurst was there to greet me and led me to a table with silver salver and teapot, sandwiches and cakes, which looked just like I had thought a governor would enjoy.

My hostess greeted me warmly and immediately we were joined by the Governor and a personal assistant. As soon as we sat down the Wakehursts asked how things were in the UK and in the US and Canada; they wanted news of Dr Buchman, whom they had not met, but with whom they had corresponded.

When we had finished tea and the tray had been carried away, Lady Wakehurst turned to me; "You said on the phone that you had a message from Dr Buchman."

I hesitated, wondering how to embark on the subject of the guidance of God in Government House. Then I took the plunge and burbled on about the importance of listening to God, how I had been seeking it for some years and how important it had become in my life. "In fact," I added, "Dr Buchman said it was very important that you learned to listen to God."

"That's marvellous," said Her Ladyship; "Frank and I have corresponded about this for some time. Please tell me your experience."

So I told them how I had first faced standards of absolute honesty, purity, unselfishness and love; how I asked God to guide my thinking and had sat quietly with paper and pencil writing down the thoughts that came to me. Of course I added, many of those thoughts had little to do with God, but it was important to get clear of everything that was jumbling my mind so that God might have a chance to put something in there. Then, as I sat for ten minutes or so longer, frequently thoughts came to me such as I had never had before and which, if I had the courage to act on them, resulted in something miraculous happening in my life or in someone else's.

The Governor and his aide were sitting politely listening. Lady Wakehurst turned to the aide and said, "Would you be so kind as to fetch me some paper and a pencil? I want to try this listening."

He left and came back and handed around paper and pencils, keeping some for himself. We sat quietly for a time, then each in turn read out what they had written. What they wrote of course remains confidential.

I have never met with them again. In a few weeks the Wakehursts left Australia for Northern Ireland where Lord Wakehurst had been appointed Governor. His service over several years in that

very troubled part of the United Kingdom was
remarkably peaceful, and I have often wondered
whether it resulted in any way from listening for
God's direction.

A few days later I met Charlie Morgan, the
Labour Member of Parliament for Bankstown,
Sydney and we took to each other right away.
He had started life as the son of a miner, won a
scholarship to Sydney, where he studied law and
now, in addition to being an MP, was senior part-
ner in a law firm dealing largely with trade union
cases. He was also an outstanding athlete and had
run in the Australian team. He was similar to me
in one respect – he had become the bane in the life
of the Labour party, full of ideas, forceful in his
convictions and often proving difficult with his
colleagues. I fell into the habit of visiting his office
nearly every day and he often took me to meet
people in his constituency. I learned a lot from him
about what was going on in the country.

Morgan was especially concerned about the
future of a large company in his constituency. The
Clyde Engineering works, which had prospered
through building railway engines during the time
the Japanese had threatened coastal shipping, was
now facing big cut-backs as shipping was resumed
again. The company was facing strikes and sit-ins
by the union, which resented the business slow
down. Charlie had sympathy for both management
and labour, as did I. In my time of quiet one
morning, as I was thinking about this situation, I
had a strong feeling I would like to meet the trade
union leaders and convenor of the shop stewards
and tell them about experiences I had had.

Charlie invited them to his house for supper. Among them was Bill Dryden, the convenor, a Communist. I had been told that he was totally closed to any reasoning. He arrived with the union branch secretary and I found them to be quiet, decent men, at a loss how to help their mates in this difficult situation. After I felt I had begun to gain their confidence I asked Dryden bluntly whether he was a Communist. He looked surprised and flatly denied it, adding that he had never met any Communist and had no use for their literature, which he felt was too complicated. Then why, asked Charlie Morgan, did Dryden always bring in their party line and cloud issues with division and politics?

"Do I do that?" asked Dryden. "I had no idea. I'm a boiler maker without much education. When I have to address workers or newspapermen I get help from our canteen manager and he writes my speeches for me. I don't think he's a Communist. He certainly never tells anyone he is." (Later we found out that the canteen manager had been a Communist for years.)

I then asked Dryden what he thought of the general manager, Fischer. "Oh, he's all right. He knows our position; he takes a hard line; he's very tough, but straight and good at his job. We can work with Fischer. He has his troubles with his chairman and the other directors."

The evening ended with all of us as friends and trusting one another.

Next morning I rang Charlie Morgan, told him I'd like to meet Fischer and asked if he could arrange a lunch. He called me back later in the morning and said to meet him and Fischer next day for lunch. Over a good meal we chatted and I got Fischer expressing his views about the factory, its troubles and the people he had to deal with. I asked specifically about Dryden. "Oh, he's a decent enough fellow, but very difficult, like all those Communists."

I told him that Dryden liked, respected and trusted him. Fischer rounded on me and asked how I knew anything about Dryden. I told him of my meeting with him and his friends. Fischer asked sharply, "What are you, a snoop? Life's difficult enough without you sticking your head into the business."

"He would like to meet you socially," I told Fischer and went on to explain that Dryden was no Communist but that his speeches were being written by someone who might be. Fischer sat back, thinking, and finally said he'd let me know whether he wanted to meet Dryden. In any case he'd have to talk first with his directors.

Next day he rang Charlie Morgan to say he'd decided it could be helpful to meet Dryden, but not alone. He wanted Purves, his chairman, with him. Charlie promised to sound out Dryden and received a similar response from him – he would come, provided he could have some union men. The following evening proved to be an historic one for company and union. Charlie had arranged a buffet supper in his home. The atmosphere at the meal was a little cool, but afterwards everyone sat in a circle and I was called upon to act as informal chairman.

I began by outlining the difficulties, as I had

heard them from both sides; both sides agreed in principle with my assessment. In a nutshell, I said, the situation is that with the lowering of demand, business is falling off; the company feels it must reduce its manpower if it is to survive. The union insists it must defend the livelihood of its members and feels management is not trying hard enough to create new demand. There was a general nodding of heads.

"So let's try an experiment," I went on. "Let's sit quietly for ten minutes, each man with a paper and pencil, and each write down his thoughts, then read them out when we've finished writing." Somewhat sheepishly they all agreed.

When everyone had finished writing one of the union men raised his voice: "Why can't we sell engines to India? They've been having terrible losses during the war and they have a huge railway system. Have you tried that market?"

Chairman Purves responded, "I've been there with our chief salesman and they won't deal with us. Their government will only deal with socialist states. It's quite impossible."

Undaunted, Dryden chipped in: "I had the thought that the union needs to take as much responsibility for sales as for anything else. Could we send a union delegation from Clyde Engineering to India and see how we do?"

"Would you go, Dryden?" asked Purves.

"Yes, but I would need Mr Fischer with me, and it would be a help if our union secretary Williams came along too."

"Good," said Purves. "I'll lay that on. You get your passport and injections – our sales manager will tell you what's needed. I'll see how soon we can make the arrangements for the visit. Believe me, if we can increase demand, even if only for a short time, we can then slim down the company slowly enough to give time for the men to find other jobs. Nothing would please our directors more."

The delegation went to India and was able to secure sufficient orders to tide the company over. The deal also helped Indian railways tide over their shortages until their engine factories recovered from their wartime problems.

I received an invitation to stay in Melbourne and since the ship was still idle I was able to accept. I flew with a British army friend John Smeeton in a small Ansett Airways plane with a dozen seats, hopping from one county airport to the next. It reminded me of a rural bus, picking up and dropping off passengers and parcels, chickens and whatever. The pilot sold tickets, refuelled the plane and acted as guide and commentator on matters historical and geographical. It was just the right way to see a country. But I was horrified by the miles of dead tree stumps amidst dry, empty bush, punctuated from time to time by a beautiful green farmstead or township.

When we landed in Canberra John and I were told there would be an hour and a half delay, so we took a taxi for a tour of the city. It did not take long; in those days it was still largely a planner's dream There were government buildings along with housing for its workers, but around them were miles of wide avenues and roads with no buildings. We walked around the buildings and saw the residences of government ministers. As we came up to one garden gate John said, "This is the home of the Prime Minister."

I looked across at the house and said enviously, "I bet he's having a cup of tea this time of day."

John smiled at me and said, "Let's see if he'd like to give us a cup."

He looked as if he meant it and I protested, "You can't burst in on a prime minister and ask for a cup of tea!"

"I don't see why not; he's a widower and must spend a lot of time on his own. He might welcome company. Come on, we can but ask."

I followed John up to the front door and watched incredulously as he rang the bell. When a maid opened the door John asked, "Is Mr Curtin in? I have a visitor from Britain I'd like him to meet."

"What name shall I give?"

"My name is John Smeeton. He doesn't know me, but I am from Papua New Guinea and I'm in the army."

The maid asked us to wait a minute, then returned almost immediately and said, "The Prime Minister wonders if you would like to join him for tea in the garden."

John and I grinned at each other. "Thank you very much," said John, "we'd love that."

We were escorted through a beautiful house into a lovely garden. An elderly gentleman was sitting in the shade of a huge tree. Mr Curtin greeted us cordially and began asking many questions. He seemed fascinated to hear what I had to tell about my time in Malta, about the United States and my

voyage to Australia. He asked John about life in
Papua, where his British family had lived for
several generations. My eye was on the clock as
we chatted away in a leisurely fashion over tea and
I finally broke in with a question: "Sir, what is the
single most difficult thing that a prime minister has
to do?"

Curtin smiled. "That's easy to answer – my in-
tray."

He went on to explain; he sat down at his desk
each morning with his in-tray on his desk piled
high with documents awaiting his decision. The
first one he looks at is maybe about some foreign
affairs matter in a country he has never visited and
about which he knows very little. On the text is
written a recommended answer, pencilled by a civil
servant who deals with this country.

"I ask myself, how much does this man really
know? How much of the information he has
received from this country is correct? Is there
someone along the line who has something to gain
out of this? Will my decision set a precedent for
the next generation that will bring great trouble?"

So, said the Prime Minister gravely, he decided
either to send it back for further information or to
ask to see the ambassador of that country. The
next matter to be dealt with might be to do with
the upcoming budget: what taxes do we increase,
what will the economic situation be in the country
twelve months from now? If the war ends, what
finances will be needed to get the country back on
a peacetime footing? Has the Minister of Finance
got it right?

Our host peered at us; "So many things," he

said, "I just have to risk or take a guess and hope I'm inspired."

I said, "Phew! I never thought of a prime minister's work that way. I've been critical of politicians all my life, but in future I'll have more understanding. Is there no way to make things easier for you?"

"Oh, I've told you about the worst cases. Most of what comes across my desk is routine. Fortunately I have a private secretary who has a nose for suspicious matters. If he has a question he puts a special mark on a paper and I usually send it back for checking. He's usually right, an inspired man."

We had to leave to catch our plane. Mr Curtin sent us off in his official car. It had been an illuminating time for me. I came to the conclusion that which party is in power matters less than the quality of the men who run the parties. I felt that this prime minister had three qualities of top importance for men in his position – humility, diligence and inspiration.

In Melbourne I was eager to see a man whom I had met back in England. Ivan Menzies was a household name in Australia, the leading man in the D'Oyly Carte Opera Company, which had made popular tours through Australia. His life, like mine, had been turned around by Moral Re-Armament. He had not only enchanted great audiences by his performances on stage, but had also made a powerful personal impact on many individuals as well as business, union and political leaders. I had heard that his tour of Australia had finished, but he did not have high enough priority in wartime to secure a passage back to the UK.

I found him living alone in a one room bungalow atop the Dandenong Mountains and we had a marvellous couple of days sharing news and finding together renewed purpose for our lives. We agreed that the Australian public, so far removed from the fronts of the war had little grasp of its significance for the world.

He was given an opportunity to put issues in perspective for a distinguished audience a few days later. Ivan arranged for me to join him at an impressive farewell luncheon being given for him by leaders in many areas of Melbourne's life, headed by the Premier of the State of Victoria. I found myself sitting between the chairman of the Trade Union Congress and the editor of the leading newspaper, the *Melbourne Age*. It was an opportunity for me to learn much about Australia and at the same time to slip a few new ideas into their thinking.

When Ivan spoke, he kept them all laughing, but also gave them a philosophy for unity and teamwork. At that time the country was plagued by a series of lightning strikes. The war in Europe was almost at an end and the war in the Pacific still seemed distant to many people. They had already begun to relax into easy going ways of peacetime and commercial and industrial production were dropping alarmingly.

On my return to Sydney I found work was starting to pick up for us. Cruisers, battleships and destroyers were arriving from the UK to join the Pacific fleet preparing to attack and occupy the main islands between Australia and the US fleet. They called at Sydney to revictual and take on fuel oil, top up their crews and tune up for action. As they arrived they sent us their orders for stores by radio telephone; the stores were then loaded on to landing craft, ready to be delivered to them in Sydney Harbour. The naval ships came in spasmodically, a few at a time, and in between heavy activity I was able to visit my MP friend Charlie Morgan most days and keep in touch through him with national affairs in Australia.

Very soon VE Day arrived – Victory in Europe. The Australian government had considered carefully how the event should be recognised and decided that there would be no official celebrations. The government was afraid many people would regard it as marking the end of the war, a dangerous attitude with Japanese troops still not very far north in the Pacific; so in Australia VE Day would be just another work day. The decision was followed by a signal from the Admiralty to all our naval vessels that there would be "no dressing of ships", that is, no flying of our flags or blowing of sirens.

To me this order seemed wrong. It was highlighted for me by a telegram which reached me for delivery to Chapman, one of our quartermasters. It came from his wife; a V2 rocket bomb had landed on Woolwich, a London suburb, two days earlier and had blown off both her legs; she had sent a typical cheery Cockney message to her husband: "have lost my legs, but not my life or my love for you. Get your own back on the Japs."

That decided me. Our ship was not precisely

Royal Navy, although related to it. I decided that
the Admiralty signal did not apply to *Fort Wrangell*. I ordered full dress for the ship; we hoisted
every flag we could lay our hands on and told the
steward to lay on a banquet. Chapman, the man
who had received the message from his wife, got
a little drunk, "borrowed" a landing craft and
toured at full speed all over the harbour, shouting
to everyone through a loud hailer, "I'll show you
how to celebrate beating the bloody Germans,"
and launching into wartime songs at the top of his
voice.

All this was soon reported to me, but I did not
rush to send a landing craft to chase him; "Let
him get it out of his system," I thought. Eventually
Chapman misjudged his distance and finished high
and dry on a sandbank. Unperturbed, he kept the
engine going full speed, singing at the top of his
voice. No damage was done and eventually I
despatched a craft to bring him back, roaring with
laughter.

During his escapade Chapman had executed a
couple of turns opposite the Naval Control Office
and I awaited some repercussions. Eventually,
during a call about another matter from Naval
Control, a very senior officer said with tongue in
cheek, "Could it be true that contrary to Admiralty
orders you dressed ship overall on VE Day and
sent one of your landing craft to alert everyone
about it?"

I hesitated before answering, "Yes, that is close
to the truth."

"Oh good; I'm glad someone read about Nelson's putting his telescope to his blind eye and

doing what he thought best. I wish I'd thought of doing the same, but thanks anyway; it did our morale good."

One fine windy day we had orders to go to sea for a series of gunnery trials. It was a great relief to get out of the warm atmosphere of the cove into the fresh wind and white horse waves. The trial consisted of our anti-aircraft gunners firing at a drogue – an elongated sock – towed by an aeroplane. The gunners had to practice "eye-shooting", estimating the distance ahead of the drogue at which to aim their guns, whose platforms were bouncing around on the waves as the ship went through twists and turns.

We also had to practise shooting our single six-inch defence gun as close as possible to a target set up on a barge being towed several hundred yards behind a naval tug. This is a highly skilled operation, since both the gun and target are moving around with the motion of the sea. Our chief petty officer fired only one shot, missing the target but sinking the barge! So ended our gunnery trials.

As we were steaming back into the harbour we were intercepted by a fast naval launch which signalled it wished to come alongside. A smart naval rating ran on to the bridge and handed Captain Buster a signal. He opened it, read it and turned to me. "Here, Foss, look at this. For some unknown reason they want me to go to Canberra."

I read the note and saw it was signed by Norman Makin, Minister for the Navy. Norman Makin – this was one of the three names Frank Buchman had given me to look up! Then I noticed that the telegram was not addressed to the captain, but to me. I diffidently pointed this out to Buster, who glared at me and wanted to know what the Navy Minister wanted with me.

"Are you an undercover agent or something?"

I told him I hadn't the vaguest idea. The telegram ordered me to report immediately and the coxswain on the launch said he was waiting for me to accompany him.

I changed into my best whites and boarded the launch, which swept me to Circular Quay. As we came alongside it was evident that something was amiss. Usually at that time of day there was a bustle of ferries leaving and arriving. Now there were none. The coxswain could give me no reason. On the Quay a naval car was waiting to drive me to Mascot Airport, where I was switched to a small navy transport plane which took off immediately.

Awaiting me at Canberra airport was my friend Charlie Morgan and on our way to the Parliament buildings he told me a little of what was afoot. Navy Minister Norman Makin, who was also Deputy Prime Minister, and a highly talented man who later became first President of the Security Council of the United Nations, wanted to consult me about a strike which was crippling the country.

My heart sank into my boots. What the hell could I do or say to help these talented government people? On reaching the Parliament we were taken straight to the Cabinet Room, where I was introduced to Mr Makin, Mr Eddie Ward, Minister for Extra-Territorial Properties, and Mr Arthur Calwell, Minister for Information.

For half an hour we sat drinking tea and conversing in generalities. Then Makin turned to me and said, "Now I'd like your thoughts about these strikes and see whether you can help us come up with a solution."

"Why me?" I asked.

"Because we've seen your influence on Charlie Morgan. He used to be the bane of our lives; now he's completely changed and is one of our soundest and most helpful members."

Charlie sat with a big grin on his face.

Makin went on to say he had called him in to help about the strikes and Charlie had suggested that I should be consulted. I sat there wondering what in the world I could say. Then I recalled the mission Buchman had given me in Los Angeles: "Tell these people (of whom Makin was one) how you get guidance from God."

Now that the opportunity had arrived I felt scared stiff, but I launched in: "The only thing I did for Charlie was to teach him to listen to God for guidance; the rest followed naturally. I think that may be the only thing we can do now in this crisis."

These cabinet ministers outlined for me the history of the strike to date. The steelworkers had been organised by a man named Ernie Thornton, an avowed Communist. Recently another leader had emerged, a man, if I remember rightly, named Origlasso, who had organised an anti-Communist union with considerable success. Both men held sufficient power to threaten management that if the employers negotiated with the other's union they would pull their own union out on strike. Management had met both unions and as a result both sides had called out their members. The Communist workers had supported Thornton and most of the non-Communists had supported Origlasso. As a result work had come to a standstill in the industry, endangering the Pacific war effort.

Then Morgan and I sat in quiet with these three cabinet ministers for about half an hour, writing down the thoughts that came to us. When we told each other what we had written, one of the ministers read out: "Wouldn't it be strange if this whole business was a fiddle between Thornton and Origlasso to bring the country to a standstill, with Origlasso being an undercover Communist, to halt the Allied advances in the Pacific and so give the Russians a chance to get troops from Europe into the Pacific and so maximise their advantage at the end of the war?"

We talked a lot longer without coming to any conclusions and still bewildered, I caught the plane to Sydney. But I learned later from Charlie Morgan that after I had left, Mr Makin decided to take seriously the thought about conspiracy between Thornton and Origlasso. He contacted Herne Bay, where naval officers were awaiting posting, and selected six of them to track the two union leaders. They eventually caught them in a back room in a pub in Charing Cross, Sydney, planning together their next moves to keep the country's industry at a standstill.

As a result, the government banned both unions and insisted on new elections, supervised by the Trade Union Congress and the government. New leaders were elected and on the next day the strike came to an end.

11

Streamlining for combat

Orders came for me as gunnery officer to go to
Warwick Farm, a huge holding depot for naval
crews, to select twenty-four men to man our anti-
aircraft guns before we headed north into the
Pacific war zone. I was determined to find not only
good ratings for the safety of our ship but also if
possible men who were also good football players.
I had learned over the years that ships with a good
football team tended to have high morale.

I came across a group of soldiers at the depot
who had fought through the Western Desert, Italy
and into Southern Germany and had then volunteered for service against the Japanese and been
sent to Australia. They were obviously the kind of
men we needed. They also had had training with
Oerlikon and Bofors guns, some of them in action.
At Warwick Farm they had gone through rigorous
training for work at sea.

Their arrival aboard *Fort Wrangell* brought a
new element into our life. They were more sea-
soned and much tougher than the rest of the crew,

but fitted in well and were welcomed. Of course
they brought a few problems along with them. One
night around two a.m. the duty officer woke me,
saying there was an urgent phone call from Naval
Control. Cursing, I stumbled to a phone and was
told there was a complaint from a RNVR officer
that he had been threatened by three soldiers off
my ship that they would throw him into the harbour. I was ordered to investigate this breach of
discipline, deal with it and report back to Naval
Control.

The night watchman gave me the names of three
soldiers who had come aboard recently. I asked if
they were drunk. "Not drunk, sir, but maybe
merry and full of song and laughter." I left word
for them to report to me at nine a.m. Promptly on
time there was a knock on my door and the three
filed in and stood at attention. "For God's sake,"
I said, "sit down. This is not the army, not even
strictly the navy. Help yourselves to a cigarette and
tell me what happened."

They were all ex-sergeants in the Guards, first
class men and veterans. They grinned and one of
them told how they had missed the last liberty
boat and had to wait for half an hour for a special
boat. So they had stood around quietly singing and
joking.

I interrupted; "I've never heard you fellows
doing anything quietly."

"We were quiet, sir, until a snotty little fellow
came down the jetty and began bossing us
around."

This little fellow, they said, turned up in pyja-
mas, with a navy greatcoat with two wavy bands

with green in between on his shoulders. He had yelled at them and they had politely suggested they give him a swimming lesson unless he shut up.

I sent them to their quarters, telling them they were confined to ship with extra duties. They stood to attention, saluted and marched out.

Later that day a commander at Naval Control phoned me, asking for details of the incident and what action I had taken. I swallowed hard and told him.

His response: "Are these men who fought through to Germany and re-mustered to help beat the Japs? If so, wasn't I being a little harsh to confine them to the ship?" He added that the lieutenant who had put in the complaint had never been in action, was a paper-pusher. I suggested that I put the soldiers on liberty ship guard.

"A brilliant idea," replied the commander. Liberty ship guard involved their accompanying the liberty ship to shore, with two of them having free time on shore. As word went around among our whole gunnery crew it assured their full loyalty; besides that, the three were among our best footballers.

After my return to the ship a suggestion was made to me by some of the Australian friends that some influential people would welcome my transfer to civilian work in cities around the country, fighting to raise morale and production. I thought about the offer, but felt in my heart that this was not the job for me. My feelings were reinforced when early one morning I had the clear conviction, "You must go to Japan." I was clear in my mind that I should stick with *Fort Wrangell*.

At last we received orders to join the Pacific
Fleet at Manus, an island north of Australia that
had been converted by the Americans into a huge
naval base. Our route would be up the east coast
of Australia inside the fabulous Barrier Reef. I had
visited the Reef thirteen years earlier, swimming
with a tube in my mouth so that I could keep my
head below the surface to see the beauty of the
coral, with a friend watching out for sharks; that
was in the days before scuba diving equipment
had been developed. This time I had to be more
concerned with navigation than with the beauty of
the Reef.

In the great coral reef, extending nearly a thousand miles, there is a break known as the Jomard
Gap through which deep draft vessels can sail. At
this time it was not easy to find as the reef on
either side lies only feet below the surface. The
narrow channel is more easily seen on a rough
day, when it shows up as a calm between lines of
breaking waves.

The day we arrived there was a flat calm. We
had only celestial sights with which to fix our
position within a few hundred yards, not accurate
enough for this narrow gap. I was responsible for
the navigation and was vastly relieved when we
made the passage safely. Later, the Americans
solved the problem in typically practical fashion
by running a landing craft on to one end of the
reef and an old supply ship on to the other, thus
marking the gap very clearly.

The scene at Manus was an eye opener. There
were more naval ships at anchor than I had ever
seen before, with small craft buzzing in every direc-

tion, and on the island what seemed like miles of warehouses. We entered discreetly and anchored some distance from the US Naval ships. We seemed to be the only British flagship there. Soon we were asked if we needed help. I told a stores officer that we had trouble with one of our LCVP's (Landing Craft Vehicle Personnel) engines. Some idiot had broken a distributor cap and I asked if it could be replaced. It was an excellent petrol driven American machine. I was given the procedure and took our LCVP with us in a landing craft, together with a coxswain, to the stores quay.

We walked ashore and came on a long row of jeeps beside a notice reading, "If you need stores take a jeep and drive to the Catalog Shed." So we took a jeep and followed signs to a shed, some half a mile away. Sitting behind a counter was a black sailor, reading. When we told him what we were seeking he looked through a great tome and gave us a number. I thanked him and asked about this great complex.

He explained that the navy had sent ten thousand Seabees, the naval construction workers, to build the facilities, including the stores, homes, rest homes and a huge cinema for the fleet. The enterprise, so much larger than anything we were accustomed to in Europe, staggered my mind. We drove to Shed 156 and another black Seabee greeted us warmly, hunted through the catalogue and directed us where to find the shelf and numbered box in this huge building. We located the box, only to find it empty.

Our helper apologised, suggested we get a whole new engine, and directed us to the correct engine shed. Once more a cheerful Seabee greeted us, but when he looked up his catalogue, shook his head and told us that gas engines were now no longer allowed in landing crafts because they had been found too dangerous and had been replaced by diesels. So, take a diesel, he said. I explained that would be no use to us since our craft had two engines, the other one a gas engine.

"No problem," grinned the Seabee. "Go to the landing craft pool and get yourself a new landing craft. They have thousands of them." And that is exactly what we did. I took off with the craft, marvelling at the industrial might of the United States, geared up to win the war at whatever cost. Our arrival back at the *Fort Wrangell* with the craft boosted everyone's morale.

The first Commonwealth ship to join us was a cruiser of the New Zealand Navy. Her captain came aboard and had lunch with us, enjoying a superb curry prepared by our Goanese chef. Over the meal he talked about the British participation in the Pacific war. The Americans had more than a thousand ships here, he said, while our fleet, when finally assembled, would only include five carriers, five battleships, twelve cruisers, some ten baby carriers and around forty ancillary vessels, a total of some eighty-five. "The only possible reason for our being here," he added, "is political, so that we can have our share in the victory."

After a couple of weeks we received orders to proceed to Eniwetok in the Marshall Islands. It was later to achieve fame as the atomic testing ground, but was unknown at this time; I spent half an hour finding it on the map. Our arrival was made interesting by the semi-intoxicated state of the pilot who boarded us to direct us into the lagoon. He brought us in safely and spent a heavy night with our captain. We were the only British ship in Eniwetok.

During the lull after our arrival the Serang, head man of our Indian crew, came to me for help. He had received a letter from his number-one wife asking him to sign some papers to permit his proxy wedding to a third wife. She had written that she was getting older and needed help in the home. The proposed bride was the nineteen-year-old daughter of her sister, who had recently died; as he could now well afford to have a third wife, he should do so. Slightly out of my depth, I asked what the girl was like. He said he'd never met her, but his first and second wives would have consulted together and he trusted their judgment.

When I said that no English women would put up with this kind of thing, Serang agreed that he'd heard that, but thought it was stupid, with so much work to be done around a house, too much for one wife to cope with. "No Asian woman," he added, "would tolerate the tyranny of monogamy. Women are in a much stronger position to deal with a husband if there are two or three of them. One may be an expert cook, another very good with children, and maybe a third is good fun. You can love them all, and they're all happy."

What more could I say? I helped him fill out the forms and arranged for them to be flown to India via the USA. When I returned home and told Nancy about all this her response was; "There's something in it." So I asked her to select a second wife with whom she would feel at home! And from time to time would point one out to her. But no one has ever risen to the challenge; Nancy has been condemned to my tyranny, and I to one wife – and I've loved it!

In due course the *Tyne*, a Royal Naval "mother ship" arrived at Eniwetok. A mother ship is one that provides such services for smaller ships as repair workshops, recreational facilities and sick bays. Then came destroyers, some Australian minesweepers and a mini-carrier. Soon after they were all at anchor we received a signal that all British ships were to report to the *Tyne* for a conference next morning. As signals officer all signals came to me and I was supposed to deal with them, only passing on their contents to Captain Buster. In these signals was an order to draw alongside an American tanker at the other end of the atoll and fill up completely with bunker fuel.

When I told Buster about this order his reaction was, "We'll attend tomorrow's conference, but we don't need to fill bunkers, we have nearly a thousand tons already."

I argued with him that we had no idea of our ultimate destination and might well need full bunkers. It emerged that his real concern was that he had had no experience of laying a large ship up against another. Admittedly it was a delicate operation, with the danger of the tanker at anchor swinging around in a puff of wind and colliding with us.

"I might make a mistake," admitted Buster, looking up at me sadly, "and cause damage or even kill someone."

Being young, brash and conceited, I told him I'd performed the operation many times when I was at Pangbourne Nautical College – something every cadet had to practice until he had it by heart. "Besides, the bigger the ship, often it's the easier to handle, less affected by wind and tide."

Buster asked if I could handle it; I nodded and set about the job. In fact it went very well indeed; it was a calm night and I never put the engine more than dead slow ahead for a few seconds at a time, lined up the tanker and moved alongside ten feet apart. We put ropes fore and aft and drew the ships alongside with our winches. We finished up with our bridge right alongside the bridge of the tanker. When we finished the manoeuvre we were close enough for the two captains to greet one another. The American congratulated Buster on a beautiful job – never seen a better landing. Buster replied in an unconcerned manner, "Not bad, was it?"

Next morning Buster was in my cabin by eight thirty, very early for him. He said he'd been awake all night worrying about this upcoming conference. "I want you to come with me. I know nothing of RN procedure, signals and the rest. They'll probably ask me questions I can't answer. This naval rigmarole scares me."

When I protested that the signal had said "commanding officers only," Buster ordered me to accompany him. We proceeded to the flagship and headed for the conference room. At the door I was stopped from entering by two marines. Buster, with his four gold bars flashing in the sunlight, ordered them to let me pass. When a corporal tried to argue, Buster froze him with, "I take full responsibility."

The conference had already begun and when the admiral set eyes on me he whispered to a lieutenant-commander, who approached me, still standing, since there was no chair left for me. We recognised each other – we had been at Pangbourne together. Buster ordered him to get me a chair; the admiral nodded and I was seated. The admiral went on to announce that a major move was being planned to advance directly towards the Japanese mainland. That required "storing the fleet at sea," and we were the core of a logistic support group to work together to meet the various needs of the task forces.

He turned to Buster, "We have been discussing the essential communications of the operation, especially with VHF radio communication. Now, *Fort Wrangell*, do you have TBS?"

Buster, looking confused, turned to me and I whispered "Yes."

"Yes," declared Buster.

"What ranges?" asked the admiral.

Buster looked even more miserable, and I told him the ranges, but before Buster could repeat them, the admiral suggested it would save time if I answered directly, if my captain agreed. Buster agreed wholeheartedly – "That's why I brought him; he's my Naval Liaison Officer."

By this time it had dawned on me that *Fort Wrangell* was probably the most important vessel present, since although all the naval vessels had their individual significant roles, without our ship on hand to re-store them, all would have to sail back to Manus.

When the conference broke up, the admiral sent for me and asked what exactly was happening on my ship.

"Sir," I said candidly, "someone in the Admiralty made a great mistake. Captain Buster is a brilliant shipmaster for Indian-manned ships, but he hasn't the remotest idea about the way the Navy works. He never should have been asked to learn all this new technology."

The admiral looked thoughtful. "We have a problem. We are planning major changes in your ship, with newly designed equipment for an entirely new style of fleet storing."

I asked what the problem was and added blithely, "We've managed so far. I'll take care of all the navy stuff."

The admiral did not look fully convinced, but admitted, "Mike (my Pangbourne friend) tells me you are a competent sort of person. There is no one within a thousand miles who has any idea how to take over this job, and we need to start operating in three days. All right, you carry on; keep me informed if you have difficulties. In wartime we have to take these risks."

For the next few days the fleet bosun, a very senior non-commissioned specialist in rigging, wire gear and ship's handling equipment, and I were kept busy designing and making new gear for storing and transferring cargo. As we worked, the basic reason for my involvement in this work became clear to me; *Fort Wrangell* was much better designed for cargo handling than was the

navy fleet's sea-issuing ship *Glenartney*, manned
by Royal Navy ratings. Although she was a much
faster steaming ship, her cargo handling was slow
because she was a "three island" ship, with raised
forecastle, midship section and stern poop. Her
crew members had to carry cases up ladders and
along alleyways.

Fort Wrangell, on the other hand, was flush
deck, like an aircraft carrier, and we put rollers on
the deck and one man could push a ton of stores
to the issuing point with ease. We also had steam
winches, which one man could operate, rather than
Glenartney's electric winches which required up to
fifty men for cargo transfer. The *Glenartney* had
achieved up to five tons an hour; the best delivery
we achieved later was ninety-five tons an hour.

There was one light moment in the midst of all
this strenuous designing of equipment and training
of crews. I was called on deck by a lookout who
pointed to a large American landing craft
approaching us. As she swung around to come
alongside I called out to the officer in command,
"Howdy, captain, what can we do for you?" I was
learning the correct way to address US small ship
men. He grinned and replied, "Do you want any
wristwatches, fountain pens or anything? I need
medicine."

I knew what he meant – "medicine" was the
code word for whisky. The American fleet was dry,
no alcohol allowed on board, but when the ships
were resting in an atoll base there was always
demand for whisky, unobtainable except from
British and other foreign ships. I didn't think
anyone aboard *Fort Wrangell* wanted anything

from him, but I invited him and his crew aboard and gave them a few drinks.

He showed me samples of the wrist watches and pens he had "for sale". I asked him where he obtained them. He looked at me incredulously and said with a big grin, "Lend Lease of course." Lend Lease, the agreement signed between Churchill and Roosevelt whereby the US would supply Britain with destroyers and the like in return for the use of some of our naval bases, was not intended to finance the acquisition of Scotch from us – but who knows?

12

Life at full pressure

At last we were ready to set off on our long journey to Japan. Our small logistic support unit consisted of our flagship, the sloop *Pheasant*, the small carrier *Arbiter*, the water tanker *Bacchus* and four small Australian minesweepers. Our immediate destination was a link-up with the large fleet somewhere in the Pacific north of the Equator.

Before departure it was decided that we would try out our experimental stores issuing system for the first time with one of the Aussie minesweepers, *Ballarat*, as soon as we were clear of Eniwetok. *Ballarat* moved up alongside us, but steamed up too far off for us to operate with so small a ship without dipping the sling of stores into the water. We signalled that she must move in to not less than a ship's length from us. Her commanding officer did not like doing this and we had to yell at him through our loud-hailer to come yet closer. His fear was understandable since there was a choppy sea and he found it hard to steer a steady course.

We managed to supply him without getting any stores wet, but there was a minor tragedy. Since she was part of the Australian Navy the crew had to pay for any luxury goods we supplied to them. The crew tied their hard-earned cash into a waterproof bag, but half way across to us the bag fell into the sea. They let go their jackstay with lightning speed and were off astern chasing the bag which was still floating, but disappearing from view in the waves. In their haste they did not give us a chance to reel in the jackstay quickly and it threatened to foul our propeller and bring us to a standstill. Luckily one of our lookouts spotted what was happening and I was able to ring "stop engines", swing the ship hard to port to keep the cable clear.

Next day we met up with our first task force. We had been warned that the huge fleet aircraft carrier *Formidable* would be reaching us at dawn. She came racing up between the lines of ships, then slowed to our maximum speed of fourteen knots. She then called us on her loud hailer, "As we have four engines we can control our speed within a very small range, but at your working speed we do not steer too well, I suggest that we keep station on you for speed and steer a straight course, and you keep the distance off us. Do you agree?"

Captain Buster was standing next to me on the bridge. Although it was my job to conn the ship, he said to me, "Certainly not. Tell them they have to keep station on us. He will control speed and steering to our course."

I looked at him wryly, picked up the microphone

and said to *Formidable*, "We agree to operate as
you suggest."

Buster exploded, "That's bloody mutiny, Foss!"

I interrupted, "No, sir, not mutiny.' I told him
I had thought earlier about what must be done
and this was the safest way. When he thought
about it he would agree.

Buster glared at me, turned on his heel and went
below and stayed there during the whole operation.

I dismissed him from my mind as I had plenty
to think about, with the thousands of tons of our
huge ships steaming so close together in windy
weather, and within aircraft reach from the
Japanese coast.

Then *Formidable* called on his loudhailer, "Be
prepared to receive our jackstay." This had been
the normal procedure, but now we had worked
out the new system at Eniwetok. So I replied
respectfully, "No, sir, I would be grateful if you
would take our jackstay. This way will work
better."

There was a growl from the carrier, and then,
"Prepare to receive our jackstay. I am firing now."

I replied, "We are ready and will try your way,
but I warn you if it is too slow we will break off
operations."

Formidable replied, "You are new up here;
we've been doing this for some months."

I replied, inwardly cursing, "OK, we will try
your way."

We received and made fast their jackstay. On
the carrier some one hundred men hung on,
moving with the roll of the ship to keep the wire

out of the water, while another gang ran across the deck with a lighter line, drawing the sling of stores across the jackstay between the ships on a runner. At the end of the first hour we had only managed to pass five tons of stores and I was fed up.

I called on the loudhailer, "*Formidable*, I intend breaking off this operation. It's too slow and we will not be able to store all the vessels today that we have arranged to supply, unless we change to the new system we have been using."

There was a growl of anger; "What do you mean – too slow? It's going quicker than we've ever experienced before."

I replied that unless we could supply them three times faster we would not complete the job we'd been sent to do.

Formidable came back in a somewhat mollified tone, "I'd very much like to see that. What do you suggest?"

"We will make our jackstay fast on the end of yours; you heave it aboard and make it fast as high up as you can and leave the rest to us."

"All right," he said; they were willing to try it.

During the next hour we put aboard fifteen tons. When she left after three hours, fully stored, *Formidable* sent the signal, "Thank you, that was very good."

At the same time, on the starboard side we had been storing ship after ship – two destroyers and some escort vessels. When darkness fell and the operation had to be stopped, with all of us dog-tired, a signal came from *Ballarat*, "How did the practice go?"

I replied, "Your training with the little fellow
highly satisfactory. With the big chap we learned
our lesson the hard way." We then received a
signal from the Commander, Fourth Cruiser
Squadron, "Good work. Nothing more tonight."

I took a little rest, but still had to stand watch
from midnight to four a.m. After that it was a
steady round of feeding ships as soon as it was
light until darkness around eight p.m. After that
we had to reform the positions of the task force
ready to continue storing the next day. While all
this was going on, large tankers were filling up
the bunker tanks of these same ships and then
themselves being replaced with fresh tankers.
seldom had more than four hours of sleep in twenty-four – but it is surprising how a ten minute
catnap can refresh you.

During the whole operation we revictualled at
least one hundred and forty-four ships, many of
them several times. On our best day we served
sixteen ships, including two aircraft carriers, one
battleship, three cruisers and ten destroyers, eight
of them before breakfast. On that day one hundred
and eighty-seven tons of stores were passed to the
various ships as we steamed along. Those stores
included meat, vegetables, dry goods, drinks,
smokes, writing materials and clothing – all of the
articles dug out from the store lockers, sorted out,
manhandled, recorded and passed across the sea.

Our Indian sailors and army "smash and grab"
gangs did a wonderful job. At the end of that day
the Commander of the Logistic Support Group
sent a signal to the Commander-in-Chief: "The
willingness and co-operative spirit shown by Fort

Wrangell has done much to make provisioning at sea a comparatively easy task."

Fortunately our labours were enlivened by some amusing incidents. As a frigate came alongside to provision I noticed that the commanding officer, though young, was totally bald. I had just read a snippet in the *Readers' Digest* about a bald man who had made his hair grow by rubbing brandy on it. I cut this out as the frigate was being revictualled and sent it across to him.

He read it, shook his fist at me, then sent a message, "I'd like to try that remedy. Do you have a bottle of brandy?" Brandy was in short supply except for medicinal use and I was guarding it carefully, but I responded to his cheekiness and sent him a bottle from my own locker.

He thanked me and steamed off to his position. Early next morning he sent me a message, "Have tried your remedy. It works marvelously but makes you bloody thirsty. Can I have a case, please?" Amidst a good deal of laughter our storesman dragged a couple of bottles from some hidden source.

When an "N" class destroyer came alongside I noted that she was part of the Australian Navy, but her commanding officer hailed us in a very upper class English accent. I replied, "I thought you were all Australians on that ship."

"Of course we are."

"But you sound true blue English."

"Oh, no, old fellah, I'm dinkie-die, dinkum-Aussie, aren't I?" He appealed to his crew around him.

They shouted, "Oh yea, true bloody blue!" And collapsed in laughter.

Another day, while we were storing a destroyer, the captain asked me if we had any cheese, other than "mousetrap." I made enquiries, but the victualling officer informed me that all we had left was one very ripe gorgonzola, overlooked at the back of a food locker. The captain decided to risk it and we sent it to him.

Next day he was duty destroyer, serving as a fleet messenger and one of his tasks was distributing copies of the Roneod fleet news. He came alongside and asked if we had received our copy, then fired a line across us with the newspaper. We opened it, eager for the latest news of the war.

On the last page was this item: "Aboard HMS. . . . in mid-Pacific. At three am today a dreadful noise was heard in the cold room and was investigated by the Master at Arms. On opening the door he was attacked by a *Fort Wrangell* gorgonzola, but bravely defending himself with a bayonet, he speared it and rushing to the afterdeck, threw it far out into the sea, which it entered with a considerable hissing and leaving behind a terrible smell."

The most memorable day of the operation for me came while we were victualling the battleship *King George V* on our port side and the destroyer *Barfleur* on our starboard. We were aware that time was of the essence since we were now not far distant from the Japanese coast. Suddenly we received a message from our senior escort, the sloop *Pheasant*, "Japanese aircraft have laid a long row of floating mines right across our bows about three miles ahead. Urgent that evasive action be taken."

This was followed almost immediately by a loud hailer on the *King George V* calling, "*Fort Wrangell*, what action do you want us to take, sir?"

I turned to our senior signaller and asked, "Why is he asking us what to do?"

The signaller dug out the book of King's Regulations and Admiralty Instructions and pointed out the order which stated that if three ships were made fast to each other while steaming at sea, the ship in the middle shall take charge of all manoeuvring.

So, suddenly I found myself with the responsibility not only of getting my own ship out of danger from the mines, but of taking care of the fleet's biggest battleship and its newest destroyer.

I called back on the loud hailer, "May I suggest that we alter course ninety degrees to port in five-degree turns?"

KG5 immediately responded with what sounded like a chuckle, "That is a bold and sensible suggestion. I agree if *Barfleur* does also." *Barfleur* agreed, and we came around to our new course well before we reached the mines and without having to interrupt our provisioning of either ship.

During our issuing of stores to another ship I saw the bravest deed I have ever witnessed. Chota Tindal, our number three Indian, was supervising the working of the port jackstay when the two ships lurched in opposite directions and the jackstay dropped close to the water. The winchman quickly took up the slack in order to keep the holdall in which the stores were being passed from going into the water. The slack jackstay caught a couple of feet under the water on a projection from the ship which protected a waste water outlet. The jackstay caught fast and the whole operation was stopped.

Without a moment's hesitation, Chota Tindal lowered himself over the side, without any safety harness, and hung with one hand to a rope, working with the other to clear the jackstay, suspended between two ships that were rolling close to each other. After a good five minutes he succeeded in freeing the jackstay, climbed up on deck and signalled for the operation to continue. All this he did without a word, as though it were just a normal part of the day's work. It was one more indication to me of the character of the Indian seamen.

When our Moslem deck crew celebrated the feast of Ramadan I was invited as their guest of honour and given the first helping of their delicious Ramadan curry. Shortly afterwards the Serang, headman of all our Indians, called on me one afternoon in my cabin and said, "Sir, here are my keys. By tomorrow morning I will be dead. I recommend that you promote Chota Tindal to take over as Serang. He is better than Burra Tindal."

I sat, flabbergasted. The man appeared well and healthy and though he was over sixty looked as though he had many good years ahead. I protested, but he was adamant and I finally accepted the keys, but said, "I'll wait until the morning and see what happens."

Next morning Chota Tindal came to see me and asked for the keys, adding that the Serang had told him I wanted him to be the new Serang. "Where is the Serang?" I asked.

"In his cabin of course, sir."

"Why didn't he come to see me?"

"Because he is dead, sir. Did he not tell you he was going to die?"

I protested that he was well and fit last night. Tindal replied, "Sir, you don't know our ways. When our time comes we just die. It's quite normal for us. I understand you have a different way among English people."

I said, "I must see for myself," but first I went to call on the surgeon, told him what had happened and asked him to go with me to take a look at the Serang.

Doc just sat there and said, "If he said he was going to die, don't worry. He'll be dead all right, from natural causes. That's the way they do it. I've experienced the same thing among the Eskimos of Northern Canada. They're very tidy and efficient, all arrangements made."

I insisted that he went with me to the Serang's cabin. There, the Indians were sitting around praying. Many of them had painted or woven in rope tributes to the Serang. There was no mourning or sadness, only affection and peace in the room. I thought to myself, we have a lot to learn from these people. Later that day we stopped the ship and had a simple burial service, turning the ship to point towards Mecca. All the sailors, watched by the rest of the crew, brought out their mats, prayed and sang. Next day life was back to normal on the ship with the new Serang in charge.

News reached us of the dropping of the atomic

bomb on Hiroshima, followed by that on Naga-
saki. For our crew it was welcome news, terrible
as the destruction might be. For us it meant an
early end to the war and the saving of countless
lives among the Allies, as well as probably among
the Japanese. For me, too, war's end meant the
end to an absence of more than a year from my
family, and months of silence, since I was receiving
no mail from home, although Nancy was writing
to me.

When we received orders to proceed to Tokyo
Bay we hoped and assumed that Japan had surren-
dered, and there was great excitement all through
the ship's company. As night fell, the chief steward
came to see me and asked if it were really true that
the war was over, and if so, did I think it would
be a good idea to give every member of the crew
a "tot" tonight?

On Royal Navy ships a "tot" of rum was a
frequent privilege, but on merchant ships crew
members could buy beer, and in some ships spirits,
at their own expense. But we had run short after
such a long spell at sea and had had none for our
crew for several weeks.

Without thinking, I replied, "That's a good idea;
it would give them a great lift after working so
hard and willingly so long. Yes, do that."

At midnight I went on watch. The helmsman
was my old friend Chapman, who had enlivened
Sydney Harbour on VE Day. He arrived singing
one of the songs he favoured when he was tipsy.
I sent him below to fetch his watchmate Barklem,
who also came on bridge in a very elated mood. I
decided that Chapman was such an "old sweat"

he could probably steer perfectly well, and I sent Barklem off grumbling to check the blackout, and settled down for an hour to watch Chapman steering, checking his course discreetly on a "tell-tale" course recorder. He was singing quietly, but held an exact course. Chapman had served as a helmsman on the *Queen Mary* until the outbreak of war and was a very skilled man.

At one a.m. he was relieved by Barklem, who steered safely, but with more effort than usual. I returned at two a.m. and all seemed well, so I went to the chartroom to lay off some courses for the entering of Tokyo Bay. I didn't know whether the Japanese would send out a pilot or whether I would have to take the ship in myself. I'd been in the room a couple of minutes when a gunnery lookout on the starboard side of the bridge came running in to say the aircraft carrier to our starboard had altered course and was coming across our bow. I shot out on to the bridge, saw the carrier and glanced at Chapman, who was leaning over the wheel, fast asleep.

We had made a slow but definite swing to starboard and were heading straight for the carrier. I yelled at Chapman; he woke and immediately started to bring the helm amidships. I yelled, "Hard to starboard" and when our bow was clear of the carrier's stern, "Midships hard to port," and we passed safely, but very close to the stern of the carrier and across the bow of a tanker.

Immediately the radio telephone began chattering on our loudspeakers: "From Nowhere (the call sign of the carrier) to C in C, Bartender (our call sign) appears to be not under control but has hoisted no signal and very nearly sunk us." Some clever young junior on the bridge was obviously banging out an irresponsible signal.

I immediately got on the microphone and said, "Bartender one to Nowhere and C in C. Have had trouble with my steering, which has been rectified and will not occur again."

After a five-minute interval, C in C came back with: "It is essential when a ship is 'not under command' to hoist the appropriate lights to warn other ships even in a close enemy situation."

The message went on quoting at length a piece culled from King's Regulations, which I knew by heart. I then posted the gunnery rating to make sure that Chapman, and then Barklem, did not doze off, and the watch passed safely. Both men were exhausted from weeks of keeping station in close formation during which the engines had never stopped.

After a while, the C in C called us to ask whether we intended to regain our station; if so, please let him know when. I replied that we would very much like to return to station, but since the fleet was proceeding at our maximum speed we simply could not do so. C in C replied that in that case he would re-form on us, since they could not afford to slow down. He gave the orders and the manoeuvre was carried out without difficulty, but of course it meant that every ship in the fleet knew of our embarrassment. It became the topic of much ribald chaffing when we reached our destination.

13

Bravos and blunders

Fort Wrangell approached the entrance to Tokyo Bay very quietly and without disturbance. Much to our relief we were met by a Japanese pilot who was no doubt as interested to look us over as we were to check up on him. He did his job and said very little. We found ourselves the oddball among the ships at anchor in the Bay; most flew the Stars and Stripes and all the British ships flew the Navy's White Ensign.

As we came in with our Blue Ensign, the Merchant Marine flag on our mast, we sailed close to the giant American battleship *Missouri*. Suddenly a signal light began to flicker from her. Our duty signaller read it aloud to me, although I could perfectly well read it myself: "What is the anchor for?" The battleship was no doubt querying the anchor depicted on the Blue Ensign.

I couldn't resist sending back: "To hold the ship when she stops."

Evidently *Missouri* was not amused. I noticed American eyes scanning us through binoculars;

then suddenly her main armament of some twelve
eighteen-inch guns swivelled round and aimed
directly at us until we anchored off the port of
Yokohama, close by the city of Tokyo.

We still had received no official word of a
Japanese surrender, but a cacaphony of American
radio telephone messages among the Americans
made it clear that they were in charge. More and
more ships were arriving and we finally were
informed that our main mission was to get together
bedding, blankets and stores to help equip the
small aircraft carriers as passenger ships to carry
prisoners of war as soon as they were released.

One morning a British destroyer called Naval
Control on the radio telephone from Ujiji asking
for berths, bunkers, stores and water for released
prisoners of war. The message was greeted with
total silence, although twice more repeated. Then,
several minutes later, an American voice shouted,
"Who in the hell is in command in this goddamm
place? This is Colonel. . . . on HMS. . . . Give us
goddam anchor berth and tell us when the stores
are coming." There was an immediate reply in a
meek voice from Naval Control giving the berth
number, saying that the stores had been ordered
and that the POW's would be collected that afternoon. "And about time," the colonel signed off. I
learned later that he also had been a POW.

Everyone aboard was aching to get ashore and
see for ourselves what things were like, so I was
inundated with volunteers as soon as we received
orders to dispatch landing craft with Bass beer into
Yokohoma. Each released POW was to be issued
with a bottle. Taking advantage of my operating

responsibility I set off as navigator on the twenty mile journey. Half way across I noticed that our Oerliken guns had not been mounted. We had no protection, should the Japanese people not have been told that hostilities had ceased, or should they be armed and decide to snipe at us. My fears were groundless; Japanese civilians met us and helped discharge the beer into trucks which had been commandeered.

One elderly man told me in English, "We on the Japanese mainland have hated the war for years and longed for you to arrive. We would have welcomed you with open arms."

Ahead of us lay a half completed aircraft carrier and as it was deserted I walked aboard and looked around. The poor quality of the work was evidence of the severe shortage of tools and materials. Close by a large hospital ship pulled in and ambulances arrived with stretchers on which lay sick POWs. They were laid on the dock and a crane from the ship was lowered to swing them aboard. However, there was no one to attach the stretchers to the hook. Standing around were men in American naval uniform and I rounded on them. "Why don't you help these sick men?"

They grinned and one of them said, "OK, mate," in a very Cockney accent. After they had helped swing stretchers aboard I asked them which ship they were from. "No bloody ship, mate. We're POWs too. When we were released the Yanks dropped these uniforms by plane."

I talked with three of them. They had been POWs in Japan and when I asked if they had a terrible time, the Cockney replied, "Oh, no, mate.

I had it very easy. When they found out I'd been
a boilerman in civvy street they put me to work in
a factory. Next to me on my shift was a lovely
Japanese girl. Right now I'm in two minds whether
to go home or not."

Another man described how he'd been a railway
shunter before the war and was drafted into the
same job on the Japanese railways. He said with
a big grin, there was a lot of corruption and he
was helped by the local mayor to shunt a truckload
of food into his prison camp, along with another
truckload into a siding near the mayor's home. In
fact, these men said, they had lived better than
most Japanese, who had suffered horribly. One of
them added, "I could never hate them. They're
basically very nice people."

We went exploring, boarding a tram to reach
the city. As we climbed aboard people offered us
their seats. We remonstrated, but they insisted. The
woman conductor refused to take our fares. When
I gave my seat to a very old lady carrying a large
bundle of sticks all the Japanese seemed very dis-
concerted, and amazed when two of our boys took
the bundle off her so she could take my seat. They,
like our own people, had been bamboozled by
official propaganda to fear the worst from the
enemy peoples. They had expected to be brutally
dominated by us and were astounded to be treated
as fellow human beings.

I visited a store and found little on the shelves,
but when I saw a typewriter I asked the price. The
young girl behind the counter picked it up and
started to offer it to me free. We had been
instructed to pay for everything, so sadly I turned

down her offer. Thousands of our men did take advantage of the situation, but soon after they returned to their ships with their loot inspectors arrived. Thousands of items were hurriedly dumped into the harbour.

During those days we were enveloped in an atmosphere of confusion. It seemed that everything had to be improvised. For example, it had been decided that the signing of the armistice should be performed aboard the *Missouri*, flagship of the US-British Pacific fleet. A senior US Naval officer came aboard *Fort Wrangell* to check whether we had a suitable wooden table on which the armistice papers could be signed with appropriate dignity. It seemed that US Naval vessels were all made of metal – "old tin tables", as the officer described them. We did indeed have a fine mahogany saloon table, but it was screwed to metal legs, welded to the deck. He could not wait around for it to be cut loose; we were glad, since we could see it finishing up in some war museum.

Another unforeseen incident in which I was involved arose out of the time-honored Royal Navy custom of celebrating a victory by "splicing the mainbrace" – issuing a tot of rum to every sailor. But Naval Regulations dictated that only the King or the Commander-in-Chief could order this. The C-in-C of the joint US-British Fleet was Admiral Nimitz, an American, and he sailed on a ship which, like all US Naval vessels, was "dry". One morning we received a signal asking us the maximum number of tots we could supply if needed. We sent back a signal indicating that at

normal strength we could supply x-thousand tots;
with dilution, considerably more.

Then came a second message: "A number of
boats from US ships will be coming with letters of
authorisation to draw tots, bringing vessels sufficiently large to carry their authorised ration.
Please supply as best you can."

All day small boats arrived and left with a considerably weakened brew. That evening we
received the awaited signal, "Splice the Mainbrace."

That same night most British ships at anchor
were floodlit as crews were hard at work painting.
Next morning those of us who had arrived looking
like rust buckets were all bright and gleaming,
ready for the official Signing of the Surrender. It
was my fate to provide a scene even more dramatic
to many than the actual Signing.

On the morning of that day we had orders to
up-anchor and proceed alongside the British flagship *King George V*. She was moored to two
buoys, fore and aft, and there was a fresh wind
blowing athwart her. She was built to lie fairly low
in the water, but had very high superstructures
running from the bow along two-thirds of her
length. By this time *Fort Wrangell* was "flying
light", with very little cargo or fuel. In this condition every manoeuvre we made was affected by
wind.

I was responsible for the "pilotage", putting her
alongside *KGV*, and I approached this task with
my customary conceit. We moved along parallel,
holding our bow up against the wind, but when
our bow went behind the lee of the *KGV* upper-

works, and no longer had the wind to keep the
bow straight, the ship suddenly swung round and
headed for a direct collision with the flagship. The
admiral, captain and several hundred sailors were
more than interested spectators.

I immediately rang full speed astern, just in time,
and we began to move away stern first, with our
bow only about ten feet away from the battleship.
On her deck several sailors were running around
with fenders to slip in between the two ships, to
cushion the impact should they touch. They were
over optimistic, since if ships of our size were to
touch, however gently, damage would be almost
inevitable.

After our ship had moved away I reshaped our
course towards *KGV*, but the same thing happened
again. By this time the decks of both ships were
crowded with onlookers and spectators with binoculars were watching from ships around us.

On the third attempt I approached the battleship
at right angles, behind the shelter of her superstructure, stopping the engines and drifting in until we
were close enough to throw two lines to *KGV* and
drag her alongside. Although this is a common
manoeuvre in a sheltered port it can be dangerous
in open water with a strong wind. To my surprise
it worked and we finished up with our bridge
alongside that of the battleship. Her admiral and
I were close enough to talk without loudhailers.

"I never thought you'd be able to make it," he
said, smiling. "Well done," and walked away.

Then I was inundated with duties. We swung
out our derricks and started passing over the stores
which had been ordered. In the midst of this

activity a British destroyer named *Whelp* came up close to our starboard and her commander yelled from the bridge through his loudhailer, "When the bloody hell are you going to deal with us? We are duty destroyer and in a helluva hurry. We haven't time to b. . . . around. Take our ropes and we'll heave ourselves alongside and get on with the work."

The destroyer had come up so fast and I had been so busy I hadn't even seen her arrive. I was not happy about his colourful language, carried on the loudhailer for all in the neighbourhood to hear.

I replied as calmly as I could, "Please sir, moderate your temper, your language and your impatience for a few minutes and you will be looked after. At the moment all my men are busy with *KGV*. When I have someone free we'll take your lines."

He started off again, "*KGV* is not duty destroyer in a hurry. Can't you deal with us first?"

"Yes," I replied, "we are completely ready for you and will deal with you first, but there have been delays with our arrival at *KGV* and there are things that must be dealt with before we can start your storing." We had received his order by signal several hours earlier.

Five minutes later two of our Indian seamen became free, took her lines and *Whelp* was warped alongside. Immediately we were made fast a young lieutenant, looking very smart in his spotless uniform, climbed aboard our ship, walked over to our ratings and began telling them to get on with the storing of his ship. Our ratings looked up to me on the bridge, wondering whose orders they should obey. I looked down from above, part amused and part annoyed, and said very firmly, "Come here, young man."

He had no alternative, since I outranked him, and came to the foot of the bridge and looked up. "Yes, sir, what do you want?"

"You may be God Almighty on your ship, but you don't count for a row of beans on this one. So go back aboard your ship and wait there until we can deal with you. You won't have to wait long."

He hesitated, gave a little grin, saluted and went back aboard *Whelp*.

I thought, "He's a keen, smart young officer, and his ship and crew look smart, too. He'll go a long way." I was more right than I knew. I asked my leading signaller to look up the name of the Number One officer on *Whelp*. It was Prince Philip of Greece and Denmark, in a few years to be married to our King's elder daughter. As I have watched him over the years it has seemed to me that my estimate of his promise I noticed in Tokyo Bay has been proven right.

As *Whelp* left to carry out her duties she sent us a signal, "From Captain D . . . , HMS *Whelp*; thanks for prompt and efficient service."

After all this excitement with the battleship and the destroyer the ceremony of the Armistice, which we could watch from *Fort Wrangell* a few hours later, seemed almost an anti-climax. Half way through that morning we heard a growing roar in the skies as a vast armada of planes flew overhead. I was told that some fifteen hundred took part in the fly-past. Since they came with no warning, and with our nerves still tight strung from the hostilities, it was a shaking experience. As I was standing on deck along came Serang; "Excuse me sir; these planes – are they ours?" he asked quietly.

"My God, I hope so! Yes, Serang, it's part of the surrender celebrations."

"Thank you, sir; I will go and put my men's minds at rest. They were very anxious."

I felt terrible. We officers had not given a thought to letting the Indians know what was going on. It struck me then how superior we whites were in our dealings with them, as though they were somehow less than fully human.

That night all commanding officers were invited to a party aboard the flagship. Captain Buster came to me and said, "You go; you've done all the work. I'd feel embarrassed." I pointed out that only commanding officers were invited. He countered that I had been in command of all naval operations in which the ship was engaged. Then he paused and said, "All right, I'll go, but only if you'll go with me." Frankly, I would rather have gone to bed as I was so bone weary, but I knew that he needed moral support.

We proceeded in the "skimmer" to *King George V*, arriving nearly a half hour after the time of the invitation, and we were watched by many guests in silence as Buster clambered up the gangway. Then, as I made my appearance on deck there was a chorus of ribald greetings such as, "Good evening, Bartender One, have you brought any hooch with you?" They all recognized me because at one time or another they had brought their ships alongside and I had been the one who controlled the operation. Once aboard, I was rushed off to the bar and made welcome.

There a naval captain came up to me and asked, "The captain of the *Fort Wrangell*?" I answered that I was second mate and Naval Liaison Officer. He looked puzzled and asked where the captain was. I looked around the wardroom and pointed him out. Unfortunately at that moment Buster was telling one of his funny stories that required standing on one leg with the other held high behind him – an odd sight in that impressive wardroom. The captain looked puzzled and asked why I was the one he had always dealt with. I answered that I was responsible for all storing operations at sea.

The captain murmured, "Now this is a little awkward, because the admiral wants a word with you in his cabin."

We went below, I waited a couple of minutes and was then ushered in to the admiral, who welcomed me warmly and congratulated me on a first class job. Then he paused, looking serious, and said, "Was it you who spliced the mainbrace the night before you entered Tokyo Bay?"

I gulped and said, "Yes, sir.'

"Who made the decision – you or your captain?"

"I did, sir."

"I thought so; and because of it you nearly sank a carrier with over two thousand men on board – men who had survived the war and could have been drowned because of your stupidity and big headedness. Only the King and C-in-C can splice the mainbrace. Even if I wanted to, I could not do so."

He paused, looking very stern, then his face relaxed and he added, "But you are very young and inexperienced. One lesson you must learn from this: It's better to be a respected bastard than a liked fool. When in command never say 'Yes' on the first asking, always say 'No,' or 'I'll tell you later.' If you make snap decisions you will in the long run kill someone."

It was a lesson that stood me in good stead over the many years I was to be in command.

Then the admiral recalled the naval captain who had been waiting outside the door and asked me to tell them about the situation on *Fort Wrangell*. Why had I been controlling the ship the last months?

I was horrified at the question and didn't know what to say. I hesitated and then said, "It's not for me to say, sir. You must ask the captain."

"I shall do that," he said, "but I want you to return to your ship immediately and write me a full account of all that has happened on your ship these last months. I want it on my desk at 9 a.m. tomorrow."

I went back to *Fort Wrangell* and hurried in to see "Doc", our surgeon commander. Then the two of us went on to call on Stewart, the supply commander. These were the two senior naval officers aboard, as opposed to merchant service officers, such as myself. I told them my predicament. Doc insisted that for Buster's sake the whole story should be told. He added, "Buster needs to go to hospital for a rest; you have no idea how the worry and feeling of helplessness have brought his health to a very low state."

He asked Stewart and me to write the factual report and he would add a medical statement that would make sure Buster was well cared for.

Next morning I hurried over to the flagship, left the two reports and returned. I was wondering whether to talk to Buster, when a signal arrived, "Duty destroyer will be coming alongside to collect one walking patient at 11 a.m. Please have him ready to avoid delay."

Buster's response to the signal was to ask whether we had any sick people aboard. We were interrupted by another signal, "Captain . . . is transferred to hospital ship *Tjitjalenka*. Duty destroyer will collect at 11 a.m."

Buster read it with amazement. "I can't go and take command of a hospital ship. I have no experience. I don't think I even have the right uniform."

I handed Buster the first signal. He said, "It can't refer to me. I'm not ill."

I realised I had to tell him everything, and I did. I added that Doc had written a medical report that would get him into a hospital in Australia for a short rest and then he would get home to England.

Buster was devastated. He rounded on me and declared he never thought I would let him down like this and drop him in the mire. All I could say was that in the long run he would come out the better because of the rest. And he did; fit once more, he returned to his old company and completed his service with them.

Since it was now peace time and I did not have a Master's Certificate, "Jock" Stanley, the mate, moved up to become master of *Fort Wrangell*. Jock said that now that the war was over he felt capable of doing the job. It was really only the Indians who were very confused by the move. For months they had been under my command, when I unofficially took over from Captain Buster. Now Stanley was boss. However, the voyage down to Australia proved quiet and restful as we headed for Newcastle, New South Wales, for drydocking and overhaul.

It was wonderful to enjoy ship's navigation lights and deck lights again and the ease of navigation with lighthouses and buoys. It was soon hard to believe that we had made our way successfully during the war years without any of the normal navigational aids of the day, let alone the sophisticated technology of the future – radar, satellite and electronic equipment.

14

Bound for home

Back in Australia my mail finally caught up with me, but I was dismayed to find no letters from Nancy. It seemed as if my long absences from Nancy had been too much for her. I had the impression from others that she was seriously considering that it was better for the two of us to go our separate ways.

I had long been anxious to return home and now I felt it was all the more urgent if our marriage was to be saved. On top of this was a letter from my brother Pat saying that some of my family wanted me to come back as soon as possible to re-open and manage the hotel which our mother had managed for many years before the war. It seemed to me that if I could offer Nancy the security of such a good position for her and Susie, it might still provide the means for creating a new home for us.

Passage back to Britain, however, seemed virtually impossible because there were tens of thousands of British servicemen and released prisoners

of war awaiting passage from Australia to the UK,
and they had priority over me. In addition, to make
matters worse, all crews of operational ships in the
Merchant Service were frozen in our jobs until
reliefs were arranged. The distances involved, some
twelve thousand miles between England and where
I was, plus the sheer size of the operation, meant
that I would be lucky to get away from *Fort Wrangell* in less than a year.

To make matters even worse, my position on
Fort Wrangell had become very uncomfortable for
everyone. The company had sent one of their chief
officers to take over from me, now that we were
to operate in peacetime and I had reverted to
second mate. This did not worry me, but the Indian
crew could not understand the change; they kept
coming to me for orders and to settle their problems, as they had for many months. Also, Jock
Stanley, now captain, and I had worked so closely
together that the new chief officer felt I was in his
way, and so did I.

The situation was highlighted for me one morning when a lieutenant in the Royal Naval Reserve
came aboard for a chat and a drink. He told me
he had just arrived in Australia from the UK as a
"stand by" in case any Royal Navy ship needed a
navigator. He had arrived a few weeks earlier and
had been told there was no need for relief navigators any more and that he would have to wait
for several months before returning home. He was
utterly bored and said to me, "You are very lucky
to have a berth on this ship. I wish I could get
something like that."

I jumped at that suggestion; the arrival of a

qualified second officer willing and able to take over from me was an opportunity not to be missed. The Navy proved willing to release him to *Fort Wrangell* and Jock Stanley agreed, but then we hit a snag. The Australian authorities refused to allow me to land on the grounds that there were too many UK personnel on shore already.

I did some hard thinking and eventually came up with what seemed a possible means to make it ashore. The one big grievance among our Indians was that they had not been issued any kind of uniform to distinguish them as part of our crew, despite their good service and courage during the time in the Pacific. When they had been ashore they had often been insulted for not taking part in the war effort, with their country endangered.

Their Serang had approached me to ask if his men could be given the same identification as our merchant seamen, a small aluminium MN badge – for "Merchant Seaman". There was no official way I could help in face of the intransigence of the authorities; however, I had cheated, borrowing badges from my British seamen for the Indians to wear ashore. I now persuaded Captain Jock to write a letter requiring that I be allowed to land to pursue this matter with the authorities in order to avoid trouble with the Indians in the future.

It worked. I was permitted to land by the Australians, much to the envy of our crew. I immediately took the opportunity to visit the offices of our sister company, P & O, who were our agents in Sydney, and notify them that I needed a passage home. My request was greeted with roars of laughter by the staff. One of them said, "And so do tens of thousands of others. You've got a hope, I don't think!"

I was now clear of *Fort Wrangell*, since my place had been taken by the naval officer, leaving me free to hunt around for something interesting to occupy me. I did not have to search far. I discovered that two of the friends I had made in Sydney, Bill and Eunice Coffey, were determined to embark on an unusual project for which they asked my help. They were concerned by the impact of the war on their country; men and women had been shifted out of their normal livelihood and neighbourhoods, homes had been broken up, accepted levels of morality had been undercut. There was an urgent need, they felt, to re-establish goals and standards, both individual and national.

Their proposal was to hold an informal conference at which the right atmosphere could be created for like-minded people to talk over these issues and help initiate the kind of Christian communities the war had been fought to preserve. It seemed a large undertaking, but I was glad to take part. I soon discovered that I had something worthwhile to offer. The Coffeys had found a hotel with some seventy-five bedrooms situated on a beautiful site overlooking the Pacific Ocean between Woolongong and Sydney in a national park.

The state of the hotel, however, was far from beautiful. It had been used as a barracks early in the war and then left vacant. When I drove there with Bill to look it over I was horrified by the giant cobwebs and bird droppings everywhere – all the muck of a place infested for several years. I asked

Bill how he proposed to get the place cleaned. He told me he had placed an advertisement in the newspapers describing the purpose of the conference and asking people to volunteer to come at their own expense to help clean up. To my amazement he said he had already received replies from a sufficient number of volunteers. They were due to arrive the following day.

Sure enough, they came rolling in; they were a very mixed bunch, but they worked hard and in a few days the hotel began to look habitable. They did more than clear up the place. One of the volunteers, for example, was a young apprentice carpenter named Ron Pitman who possessed all manner of skills. Someone arrived with a lot of rabbits – a curse in certain parts of Australia – and Ron skinned and cleaned them at lightning speed, taking their skins off with the flick of an arm.

Another volunteer was a technological student from Adelaide University, Malcolm Mackay – who later became Cabinet Minister for the Navy. Malcolm dived into the problem of mattress covers, which had been left on the beds and allowed to mildew, so that it was impossible to clean them. He had noticed that there was to be a sale of surplus army stores in a nearby town and turned up for it in a van he had been loaned. Some of us had raised money for the occasion. Among the lots at the sale was one of 750 mattress covers. Malcolm opened the bids with an offer of five shillings and it was knocked down to him.

He had been asked to secure a mincing machine if possible, but the only mincer for sale went for more money than Malcolm had. When the auctioneer announced, "One tormentor in excellent condition," Malcolm, thinking it was something that could serve as a mincer, diffidently bid two shillings and it was knocked down to him. He also acquired a number of useful articles.

When he returned next day to pick up his loot, everything was there except the tormentor. No one seemed even to know what a tormentor looked like. But when they searched the place, Malcolm came on an unclaimed mincing machine in a corner of an empty warehouse. The auctioneer gave it to him in place of the tormentor.

When it was learned that I had been assistant manager of a hotel before the war, and would become a manager on my return to the UK, I was regarded as the expert and consulted on everything, especially the stocking of the kitchen. A number of women had volunteered as cooks, but none of them had had any experience of bulk cooking, so I was kept busy. The conference opened a few days before Christmas and the lady who had volunteered her services as caterer approached me with the problem that she had no turkeys for the two hundred guests at Christmas dinner, nor indeed any Christmas puddings, mince pies and so on.

We were in the midst of a very hot sub-tropical midsummer and I had not even realised that Christmas was upon us. "Do you mean to say that you Aussies sit down to a Christmas dinner with turkeys and pudding and everything in this heat?" I asked.

"Of course, we have turkey and all the trimmings."

Once again Malcolm came to the rescue, setting off to buy turkeys, while the cooks and I scanned through recipe books and started in on preparing puddings and mince pies. It was December 23rd; in my hotel experience we had made the puddings months in advance; however, these turned out quite well.

Malcolm phoned from a nearby town that he could get five turkeys, but along with them he had to buy five geese, ten ducks and some thirty chicken, but for a very good price. "Buy them," I told him; "they will come in useful."

"Oh, by the way," Malcolm added, "please prepare a place to put them. They are still alive."

We moved the cars out of a row of garages, ready for the poultry.

On the way home Malcolm and his young assistant stopped their truck for a cooling drink and some of the poultry escaped. It took half an hour to round them up. Next morning we collected all the eggs that had been laid and then began the slaughtering, plucking and cleaning. Once again Rod Pitman was the star turn in the operation.

The owner of the hotel arrived shortly afterwards to see how we were making out. We were apprehensive, since as yet we had paid him no rent, and had he demanded it at that moment we could not have paid. All our cash had gone into the cleaning and other preparations for the conference. He walked around the building, inspecting everything, and sat down to a sumptuous tea prepared by our ladies. He talked about everything but money, then left, to our great relief.

Among those who came to the conference were a number of Papuans through the efforts of Cecil Abel, who had been born in Papua, but was British and raised in the UK. When the Japanese overran Papua the Europeans either escaped or were massacred, but Cecil was sheltered by Papuans and was for several years a rallying point for Papuans fighting behind the enemy lines. Cecil had come recently to Australia and had helped raise the funds for the Papuans to fly to Sydney for the conference.

Then a problem arose because when the Papuans came to board the plane in Port Moresby, Qantas the Australian airline, would not carry them because the other passengers refused to fly with "uncivilised natives". When the Minister for Extraterritorial Affairs was told of this, he was furious and issued an ultimatum to Qantas: "If you refuse to accept these good fare-paying passengers I will send a Royal Australian Air Force plane to fetch them, and in future all government personnel will be flown by RAAF." Qantas backed down and brought them; but the Papuans had the plane to themselves.

As the conference opened I thought to myself all these preparations have been the easy part compared with the task of seeking together the right way for a country to go. I certainly had little idea but it was remarkable how a first necessary step was taken. We understood that trust and friendship were essential ingredients of a true democracy and in the informal meetings we began to create

them by opening our hearts honestly to one
another about our own hopes, fears and failings.

If we wanted an honest and unselfish society,
with integrity and morality, we must fight for those
qualities in ourselves as a start. We explored very
candidly just how honest, unselfish and pure was
our own living, personally, professionally and as
citizens. We admitted that for most of us that
involved a lot of change. It demanded coming to
terms with the Almighty and asking for his help.

After a few days I could see many of the faces
around had a very different look. Friendships were
made that helped sustain men and women in their
battles during the next years, and a number rose
to positions of considerable responsibility in the
land.

Towards the end of the conference I received a
letter from the P & O Company informing me
that I could join the ship *Mooltan* sailing early in
January. They had managed to find a cancelled
place for me. After a very happy Christmas and
New Year I was given a great send-off to Sydney,
where I was due to join the ship in a couple of
days. I called on a family I had come to know well
and took the daughter Elaine for a long walk on
the beach. She and I had become very friendly
during my earlier visits to Sydney and I had become
increasingly fond of her.

My mind was in an uproar as we wandered
along the shore as daylight faded. Was I a fool to
try to stick with Nancy, who seemed to want to
go her own way? Here was a young woman who
I was sure was as fond of me as I was of her. Here
was a chance to make a new start without all the

hassle that would be involved if Nancy and I trie
life together again. But as we walked and talked
could not shake from my mind the thought that i
would be crazy to abandon the foundations o
sound home life for myself and for society, and fo
which I had risked my life these past years.

Elaine and I parted in good heart, both sure tha
we were making the right decision. I went aboar
Mooltan elated that in all the long period, from
December, 1939 until January, 1946, while I ha
been away from Nancy, I had never been unfaith
ful to her, although the opportunities and temp
tations had been manifold. It had been no grea
heroic achievement on my part. It had been a gif
from God, far more deeply satisfying that casua
sex.

My cabin on the *Mooltan* was shared with seve
Army officers, most of them lieutenant-colonels
The ship docked in Fremantle, the port of Perth
capital of Western Australia, and there I was sur
prised to be told there was a car awaiting me or
the quay and that a Mr Wise was in it, wishing
to show me around this capital city of Wester
Australia.

When I reached the gentleman he told me h
was the father of a young RAAF pilot I had me
at the London headquarters of Moral Re-Arma
ment. We drove slowly round Perth to see the
sights, finishing up in front of the Parliament build
ings. Mr Wise conducted me into a large roon
which turned out to be the office of the Premier o
Western Australia – Mr Wise. My host gave me
a delightful and unforgettable day before I wa
returned to my ship.

The company aboard *Mooltan* was cheerful, not only because the passengers were headed home after a long absence, but especially since many of them were POWs, released back to life from Japanese prison camps. They were much fitter than I had expected, emerging from the horrors of those camps, although there were some who would never recover.

I was given an interesting unofficial job aboard ship. The sexes were strictly segregated – men's cabins and women's cabins. Any man who wanted to be alone with a girl on that crowded ship had the choice of only one area – the narrow strip of deck beneath the lifeboats, on the outboard side. The three-foot stretch, next to a sheer drop to the sea, was safe enough on a calm evening, but if the ship lurched on an uneven sea, a number of couples might have been deposited into the ocean.

My job was to patrol the deck in the evenings and make sure there were no couples there, or if there were, to make them come inboard. There were numbers of young students of both sexes, young soldiers and some nurses. I earned a reputation among them of being a spoil sport. I just thought of myself as a life saver.

And so to England. Eager though I was to see Nancy when we docked at Southampton, I headed for Bournemouth to stay with my aunt and uncle, with whom I would be working for the next nine years. I wanted to establish some solid business basis for my life before getting in touch with Nancy. We began to plan together how to take over the hotel and refurbish it. My recent experience at the hotel in Australia came in handy.

I received a letter shortly after my arrival from the British India Company asking me to see them on a financial matter. I went up to London, to the Leadenhall Street offices, was ushered in and treated with great courtesy and appreciation.

Then Mr Humphries, the man in charge, said to me, "Now, on this small financial matter . . ."

I butted in, "Yes, I am very sorry about that. I should have settled it some time ago, but forgot all about it."

He looked puzzled and said he didn't understand.

"I presumed you were referring to the £1 I borrowed from the purser when I left the ship."

He laughed and said, "No, I am thinking about your pay for the homeward trip; you have not collected it."

I said I hadn't realised I had any to collect. I was very grateful for an early free passage.

"Oh, no, the Ministry of War Transport had you classified on board as Second Officer (Trooping) and you were on full pay." Humphries handed me a cheque and said he was sorry they could not have made it more. I deserved it.

I had remained on second mate's pay all the time I was on *Fort Wrangell*, while I was controlling the sea-issue operations. On other ships the man in my position had received a master's pay. I had neither known nor cared. The war was over and we had won. Now was the time to build the peace.

But what about peace between Nancy and me? This had been constantly on my mind since my return. I had written to Nancy asking her please to take a few days holiday on her own somewhere to consider what was right for the two of us to do – not what we wanted, but what our consciences told us was right. We had a daughter who needed united parents; the country needed sound homes and we could be part of the disintegration of the nation or part of the cure.

Shortly afterwards, Nancy wrote to me from Ilfracombe, where she had gone to stay for a few days. She told me that on Sunday she had attended a service at a Baptist chapel. The preacher was a woman who had preached about Joy. She had said, "Joy is J O Y, when Jesus is first, Others second, and Yourself last." This had stuck in Nancy's mind and she had decided that on those terms it was obvious that we should try to work together for the future.

Susie was now nine. When I had left in 1939 she was a little girl of three, with bad eyes and very ugly glasses. On my return I found that after two operations she did not need glasses any more. She was a lovely looking child with sparkling eyes.

Now, many years later, Nancy and I are still together, though we have had our ups and downs. In our thatched cottage in Somerset we entertain many friends and Nancy is a marvellous hostess. We grow almost all our own vegetables in the large garden which keeps us both busy.

It has been a joy to work together on this book.

Some other Linden Hall books

CLIMBING TURNS by Group Capt Foss, £3.95

Capt Denis Foss' elder brother tells his story –
learning to fly in Germany; service in the RAF
1932–46; bombing over Germany; command of a
squadron in Malta; creation of RAF Air Transport; a flight to South Africa; Mau Mau in Kenya.

I SIT AND WAIT by Frank Rowland, £1.50

Poems which build faith, composed by an older
man recovering from a stroke. Beautifully illustrated by Jean Bowerman.

**THE HOUR OF THE HELICOPTER
by K. D. Belden, £3.75**

'The life of faith is often less like toiling up a
mountain with a load on your back than like step-
ping into a helicopter and being lifted to a new
level of living.' Here is a book to 'inspire not same-
ness but variety, change, growth, hope and joy for
the future in a suffering world.'

FOOTPRINTS by Michael Barrett, £3.00

"In these pages I have set down experiences which have made me believe that 'there is Somebody there'; that there is a hand and a planning mind behind the current complexities of our modern world; that in the darkness of our difficulties there are stars to guide us."

WHATEVER NEXT . . . by Adam McLean, £4.50

Adam McLean's story takes him from the Firth of Forth, Scotland, to New York, Washington, Hollywood, the aircraft factories on America's West Coast, and then into the U.S. Army fighting up the length of Italy. It was for his grandchildren that Adam first wrote the tale of his adventures. Now a fuller account, interwoven with shrewd observations, reveals the freshness and humour of a born story-teller.

All these titles are available from Linden Hall, 223 Preston Road, Yeovil, Somerset BA20 2EW. Please add 80p for postage and packing.